THE BOOK OF HERBS

Growing herbs herself for culinary use, Dorothy Hall discovered their value in maintaining health and curing disease, and several years ago she started her own herb nursery.

Lecturing to interested groups and to fund-raising societies, Dorothy Hall was prompted to write this book to answer the many questions she is constantly asked: to tell people how herbs can simplify nutrition and benefit health, how they can improve not only the flavour of food but also the fertility of the soil, and how herbs can be most successfully grown.

Other cookery books available in Pan

Mrs Beeton	**All About Cookery**
Kathleen Broughton	**Pressure Cooking Day by Day**
Lousene Rousseau Brunner	**New Casserole Treasury**
Savitri Chowdhary	**Indian Cooking**
Gail Duff	**Fresh all the Year**
Gay Firth and Jane Donald	**What's for Lunch Mum?**
Theodora Fitzgibbon	**A Taste of Ireland A Taste of London**
	A Taste of Scotland A Taste of Wales
	A Taste of the West Country A Taste of Paris
	A Taste of Rome A Taste of Yorkshire
	Crockery Pot Cooking
Michael Guérard	**Michael Guérard's Cuisine Minceur**
Antony and Araminta Hippisley Coxe	**The Book of the Sausage**
Robin Howe	**Soups**
Rosemary Hume and Muriel Downes	**The Cordon Bleu Book of Jams, Preserves and Pickles**
Patricia Jacobs	**The Best Bread Book**
Enrica and Vernon Jarratt	**The Complete Book of Pasta**
George Lassalle	**The Adventurous Fish Cook**
Kenneth Lo	**Cheap Chow**
Claire Loewenfeld and Philippa Back	**Herbs for Health and Cookery**
edited by R. J. Minney	**The George Bernard Shaw Vegetarian Cook Book**
edited by Bee Nilson	**The WI Diamond Jubilee Cookbook**
Marguerite Patten	**Learning to Cook**
Jennie Reekie	**Traditional French Cooking**
Evelyn Rose	**The Complete International Jewish Cookbook**
Rita G. Springer	**Caribbean Cookbook**
Constance Spry and Rosemary Hume	**The Constance Spry Cookery Book**
Katie Stewart	**The Times Cookery Book**
	The Times Calendar Cookbook
Marika Hanbury-Tenison	**Deep-Freeze Sense**
	Deep Freeze Cookery

the book of
HERBS

Dorothy Hall

Pan Books London and Sydney

First published 1972 by Angus and Robertson Publishers
This edition published 1976 by Pan Books Ltd,
Cavaye Place, London SW10 9PG
4th printing 1979
© Dorothy Hall 1972
ISBN 0 330 24326 8
Printed in Great Britain by
Richard Clay (The Chaucer Press) Ltd, Bungay, Suffolk

Preface

Some have herbs thrust upon them, but I hope, since you have already opened this book, you are not an unwilling seeker of information on how to use and enjoy fresh herbs in the many and various ways they can be of service to mankind.

Since much of the literature on herb cultivation refers only to conditions in the cold countries of the northern hemisphere, I have written with temperate climates and growing seasons also in mind. And I have written in non-technical language, hoping this book will prove a readable, practical guide to the home gardener, not merely a reference work to be stored and forgotten in the bookcase.

Herbs are fascinating plants, each one with its own history and medieval lore, its general and specific application to health and diet, and its newer uses, most valuable to us, in natural control of soil fertility and balance and of insect and disease depredations of our food crops. Some of our grandmothers' remedies are now proving not to be so old-hat after all, and many recent discoveries confirm their basis of common sense, and of understanding and knowledge in the use of Nature's resources.

I hope I have answered here a few of the many questions put to me by visitors to my herb nursery, so that the home gardener will be able to select and grow the herbs that most appeal to him.

My thanks and appreciation are due to government authorities and to many friends who have helped with advice and technical know-how, and with whom I have most pleasurably swopped cuttings and plants and helpful hints.

I hope you get as much pleasure and satisfaction from your herb garden as I have had from mine.

DOROTHY HALL

Gordon, 1971

The illustrations in the first part of the book, Herb History and the Herb Garden, were drawn by Astra Lacis. With five exceptions, the illustrations of individual herbs in the second part of the book are taken from *British Herbs* by Florence Ranson (Pelican, 1949) and were drawn by Mrs Edith Longstreth Thompson. The illustrations of catmint, chicory, horseradish, lemongrass and scented-leafed geranium were drawn by Delia Delderfield.

Contents

Herb History and The Herb Garden

The Herbs

HERB HISTORY
AND THE
HERB GARDEN

Why Grow Herbs Today?

Herbs have been used from earliest recorded history as aids to the health and well-being of man. In the old cultures of the Middle East, Egypt and Arabia, as well as Greece and Rome, herbs were used in daily living in a variety of ways. They were used, for instance, to purify and sweeten the unhygienic environment in the great cities, where cleanliness of body was a luxury available to only a few, where sewage and drainage ran through the streets, and food was often rank or even well and truly "off". With their antiseptic properties, their pleasant perfumes and powerful stores of volatile oils and minerals, herbs were of great value, and were as readily available to the peasants and common people as to the princes and the wealthy and powerful. Since they were easy to collect and prepare, every household had at hand simple remedies for illness, ways to provide a more interesting and wholesome diet, and even dyes for their cloth and aids to their crop-growing and farming.

As late as our grandmothers' day, home remedies and potions were made from herbs picked from the garden or field and prepared in essentially the same way as those ancient Romans, Theophrastus and Pliny, and the Greek, Dioscorides, had found by experiment and inquiry to be the most suitable. With modern times and Henry Ford, this century, with the development of the petroleum and chemical industries, saw a radical change in the living habits of most of the world's "civilized" population: a move into the cities, a literal jungle of concrete and steel replacing the forests and gardens and farms; a jungle where land became so precious that no longer could each household grow its own vegetables or keep its own few livestock, and the "physic garden" gradually became just another vague memory of a childhood visit to the country cousins, who had not yet learnt our sophisticated city ways.

3

Synthetic drugs, produced in vast amounts by the world-wide chemical giants, became the substitute for natural remedies. The ease of popping a pill in the mouth was hailed in the age of convenience. There was no longer time for a modern household to be bothered with all that old-fashioned stuff. The few courageous voices in the mechanized wilderness questioning the wisdom of upsetting the natural balance of man, beast and environment, were ignored or ridiculed.

Now this attitude is gradually changing to an awareness of the very real dangers to mankind in a world polluted and poisoned with unnatural wastes. The chemical insecticides, the industrial and household wastes, even the dyes used in our toilet paper, are adding each day to the imbalance of man and nature. The individual thinking man is looking for a way out of this spiral of self-destruction. Governments, too, are beginning to listen and plan. "Bio-degradable" and "organically-grown" have become not only economic catch-phrases but rays of light on our smoggy horizon. Natural foods are beginning to replace the over-refined, devitalized packages on our kitchen shelves; conservation and environmental preservation bodies are clamouring ever louder in the lobbies; and even the mass media, juggernauting into every corner of our lives, are crusading against the polluters and drug users and abusers.

Herbs can play their small but important part in helping to restore the harmony of man and his environment. Few dwellings are so small that a pot of herbs will not fit on balcony or sunny windowsill. For those with an average-size suburban block of land, enough herbs can be grown to provide the essentials of good health and a good table, and for those still fortunate enough to have land left to farm, herbs can not only help the family's ills and chills, and brighten up the culinary front, but can be commercially valuable in increasing soil fertility, reducing insect pests and disease, and even improving the flavour and size of the vegetable crop and the general health (and temper) of the pedigree bull.

If your appetite has been whetted, now *read on!* And to you *bon appétit*, good health and happiness.

4

History, Health and Horticulture

The Ancient Civilizations

For information on the growing and use of plants beneficial to man, we can go right back to some of the earliest history recorded in the civilizations of Arabia and Egypt, as well as Greece and Rome.

The George Ebers papyrus found in the ruins of Thebes, and the more recently discovered Edwin Smith papyrus, give much information on the use of plant medicines, and Herodotus's writings tell us of the embalming procedures used about 500 B.C. He named over 700 plants in common use for all manner of purposes, and many of these are still in use today. The Greek physician, Dioscorides, in the first century A.D., applied the knowledge gained about the properties of plants useful to man, and his "herbal", one of the earliest written, is still referred to as one of the most accurate and learned in the practice of natural medicine.

In ancient civilizations, medicine was inextricably bound up with religion. All the earliest physicians practised auto-suggestion, hypnotism and psychotherapy, though certainly in somewhat different form and under different names. Natural remedies were prescribed for natural diseases, and "magic" remedies for what we now would call psychosomatic diseases and many forms of mental illness. The skills of genuine healers were sometimes assumed by charlatans and tricksters who had no training and no knowledge, but merely a convincing manner and an outstretched palm. Any fool could chant an unintelligible rhyme or sell a so-called "remedy" or "elixir", and gullible people would buy. The disrepute thus brought to natural medicines and herbs still dogs herb users today. A friend of mine who has suffered chronic illness for many years steadfastly refuses to try any simple herbal preparations on the

5

grounds that she will not poison herself with herbs and "all that mumbo-jumbo". (I have been "poisoning" myself and my family with herbs a long time now, and our health and resistance to disease is proof enough for me that Nature knows best.) Prevention, everyone tells us, is better (and easier) than cure. The beauty of using herbs daily in many different ways is that so many of them have value in building up resistance to disease; and if a disease does strike, herbal preparations will usually do good without having the side-effects of so many artificially created drugs. But enough of my pet hobby-horse and back to our history.

As the legions of Rome spread out over their conquered territories, Roman customs and way of life changed the ways of the indigenous peoples. After the soldiers came the governors and administrators, and with them the monks, who brought not only their own religious beliefs, but practical knowledge in the fields of agriculture, health and nutrition. Many herbs were carried as gifts from one monastery to another by travelling monks, and from the monasteries the people gradually gained knowledge of the many uses to which they could be put. One of the earliest forms of taking herbs in the diet was in cordials, or an infusion of the herb in wine. From these "cordials", evolved over the centuries, came the recipes for many of our present-day liqueurs. When you next drink Chartreuse or Kümmel or Anisette, give a thought to those peregrinating monks, who used their knowledge and skill in blending herbs and spices (Chartreuse contains some forty-six ingredients) into recipes still unchanged today. These cordials were drunk usually as an aid to digestion at the end of a large meal, for the eating habits of the day were such that the food was often highly unpalatable, owing to deterioration, or indigestible. It is easy to understand the preoccupation with flatulence and stomach troubles in early herbal writings of this period.

Peaceful Britain
In Britain, the real Golden Age of herbs and herb gardens

6

began in the late fifteenth and early sixteenth centuries, when the wars of the barons and knights ended and relative peace descended. With increased security, the peasants returned to cultivate the land, and the lords set out to keep up with the Joneses. Rivalry between noble families no longer flourished on the battlefield, but each now sought to outstrip the other in the size and opulence of his home and the imagination and ingenuity of his gardeners and cooks. The formal herb garden evolved from those same monastery gardens, which were often planted in the form of a cross or diagonally-crossed square. Now the wealthy set their gardeners to constructing all manner of intricate designs, seeking to please the eye by art as well as nature. Sometimes the gardens were laid out in the form of heraldic animals, or the owner's coat-of-arms, or even his initials. Francis Bacon wrote very scathingly of these practices ". . . images cut out in juniper or other garden stuff, they be for children. As for the making of knots or figures, they be but toys. . . ." And indeed they were, as the herbs grown were more for ornament than use. But the herbs grown in the kitchen gardens, and the gardens of the peasants, were most certainly for use, and were often the only physic available.

As the herbs from other lands came to be better known and more widely used, interest in the health values of British native plants was also stimulated. William Turner (1510–68) has been called the father of British botany for his work in the classification and naming of many native British plants found in the ditches and hedgerows and woodlands. These plants were now to come under scrutiny as sources of readily available herbal preparations. Nicholas Culpeper (1616–54) one of the best-known of the British herbal healers, became a physician after studying ancient Greek and Arabian medicine at Cambridge. He was a rebel—a man with a fierce antagonism towards the orthodox schools of medicine, which ridiculed his methods and beliefs. He remained poor and died penniless, having never refused help to any sufferer. The doctors criticized him not for his lack of skill or knowledge, but for the amazing number of cures he effected, claiming he must have used witchcraft: it was

7

not possible to cure so many patients! How familiar that must sound to the many practitioners of natural medicine, even today!

Culpeper's predecessor, John Gerard (1545–1612), another British herbalist, was, though dedicated, somewhat fanciful in many of the properties he attributed to herbs. He often cribbed from other writers (not always accurately), and many of his more far-fetched remedies are quoted by those opposing the use of herbs in health or sickness.

The Doctrine of Signatures

About this time, the German, Paracelsus, propounded his Doctrine of Signatures: his belief that the appearance and general characteristics of plants gave clues to their possible uses for the health of man.

Opinions about him were, and still are, divided, some hailing him as a genius, some as a charlatan. He studied the characteristics of plants and flowers, and related them to various parts of the human body. All manner of signs and habits of growth were noted as indications to possible uses: even the slow growth or the fecundity of a flower was related to treating human sterility or "over-abundance". Even the external general appearance of a plant (e.g. garlic and chives, spear-shaped, will ward off general ill-health) was sometimes taken as a sign of its properties. For the cynics among my readers: it has been found, sometimes only in the last generation, that whatever the original method of choice, and however far-fetched the theory may sound, many of the plants so chosen to heal and maintain general health do, indeed, have the required results.

One of my favourite plants is comfrey (*Symphytum officinale*), long known and used as a healing agent for broken bones and tissue damage, both internally and externally. Scientific analysis of its constituents reveal 0·8 to 1·2 per cent of allantoin, a cell proliferant, now synthetized and hailed as a "modern" miracle healing agent. You will find allantoin listed as an ingredient in many chemists' proprietary lines. Why not grow your own comfrey and have its easily assimilable healing powers available right in your own back yard?

Another example of the Doctrine of Signatures is the age-old use of willow-tree bark for treatment of rheumatic complaints. It was noted by practising herbalists that the willow often grew and thrived in damp and cold conditions, the same conditions that produce so many rheumatic complaints amongst farmers and gardeners working outdoors. Analysis has shown that one active ingredient of willow bark is salicin, which, used externally, relieves and soothes the cramping fire of "the screws".

Salicylic acid cannot be taken internally, and it was not until 1899 that a German chemist came up with the answer—a compound called acetyl-salicylic acid, most probably better known to you as aspirin. Orthodox medicine still recommends aspirin as one of the best remedies for chronic rheumatism; it not only relieves the pain, but has a positive action on the stiff and creaky joints as well.

Time and time again, science is forced to confirm the efficacy of many natural remedies. It would appear, as the Apocrypha states, that "the Lord hath created medicines out of the earth, and he that is wise will not abhor them".

French Cuisine

When anyone mentions herbs, what is the first thing you think of? I would guess many of you would say, "French cooking!" No child ever enjoys eating or drinking anything that tastes unpleasant, and as adults we naturally continue to prefer appetizing, flavourful food (sometimes at the expense of what is good for us). So the herbs most generally used were those which added some special taste or flavour to food. Medicinal herbs and many of those which were undeniably "good for us" were often bitter or very strong, and gradually they became less frequently grown and used. One of the most valuable of these, the common dandelion, is dug up and thrown out of our gardens, because, although it contains in large quantities so many of the vitamins and minerals essential for good health, it has a slightly bitter taste, and has now become only a "weed".

After the excesses of the French Court and the nobility, and the literal starvation of the ordinary people, the French Revolution brought a great change in the eating habits of all the Continental countries. Food gradually became more plentiful; but, in revulsion against the luxury or ostentation that recalled the hated aristocrats, food was simply cooked, fresh fruits and salads were picked from the fields and put straight on the table, and simple *croissants* replaced the cakes and elaborate confections of the Bourbon Court. But you can't keep a good French cook a conformist for very long, and soon fresh herbs were being picked from the fields and gardens to give that individual touch to many a simple dish.

The Napoleonic age produced perhaps the greatest number of skilled cooks, amongst whom was Grimod de la Reynière, who in 1803 formed a society of gourmets, the Jury Dégustateur, and the proceedings of this group were published in a journal, the *Almanach des gourmands*. Later, Reynière published his own cookbooks, amongst the first ever written containing recipes as such. Carême, cook to Talleyrand, started writing cookbooks in 1815, as distinct from the "household hint" type of book written previously. Women of some position (not necessarily cooks) began to write recipe books, evolving their own individual recipes (presumably with the help of a large kitchen staff).

French food today still has the character formed in the eighteenth and nineteenth centuries—simple ingredients simply cooked, with the addition of those magic touches that make French cooking the best in the world. Many of these individual additions are herbs, added to a dish at just the right moment to release the full flavour and aroma.

Contemporary Herb Usage
Most of the diseases of early times were infectious or contageous, and required medicine, not surgery. However, the many wound herbs were in constant demand, for lance and sword injuries were occupational hazards in those stirring times. Antiseptic herbs, such as lavender, lemon balm and garlic, and

10

the cleansing astringent herbs such as yarrow, were freely used, and very efficacious they were, too.

In the last World War, as in the Great War and even the Boer War, herbs were used when medical supplies were difficult to get. British housewives in their thousands were asked to gather the old "herbs of war", both the cultivated ones in their gardens and the wild herbs in the fields, and many a wounded soldier owes his recovery to the cleansing and healing oils from humble wayside plants and kitchen gardens. Lavender was gathered literally by the ton and its oil used as a surgical antiseptic in field hospitals. Nettle, with its large iron content and stimulating properties, was used freely after the loss of blood from wounds, and the debilitating wasting of immobilized limbs. Many French hospitals still burn rosemary in the wards to purify and sweeten the air, a tradition going back hundreds of years.

Since the earliest experimental work began so long ago, those who realize the value of herbs to man have been quietly and painstakingly amassing valuable knowledge. Much of this knowledge, based on years of dedicated research, can be found in books and natural health publications, more of it can be sifted slowly from the writings of other cultures, notably the Indian and Chinese. However, for the layman, English and Continental herbs (many of which originally came from other civilizations) are the most familiar plants known and used today.

Samuel Hahnemann, the brilliant exponent of the homoeopathic school of natural medicine, found yet another principle relating to herb usage. He discovered that by giving massive doses at varying strengths of a particular herb certain symptoms could be produced in healthy people, and he formed the theory that a person showing this same set of symptoms *in illness* might be *cured* by an infinitesimal dose of the same herb. Application of his discoveries has provided some astonishingly effective results in the field of natural medicine. This is an over-simplification of a very complex theory, and further reading on the subject can be very rewarding.

11

I do not think any of us can scoff at something that works, and works not only on humans but on animals as well, thus confounding those who cry "Faith Healing!" and "If you believe in something hard enough, you will be cured." Homoeopathic doses of herbs are even being used to activate the compost heap. Work done in England recently has shown that a concentration of one in ten thousand parts of yarrow (*Achillea millefolium*) added to the compost heap is the most effective "dose". I have proved this myself, and the short time taken to produce rich well-decomposed compost has been very valuable to me in my herb nursery, where all the plants are organically grown and natural compost is one of their chief foods.

In 1927, in Baker Street, London, a Mrs Leyel started up a small shop selling dried herbs and herbal preparations, known as the "Society of Herbalists". Interest in the use of herbs grew to such an extent that in 1936 a new Society of Herbalists was formed by admirers of her work, by those who had benefited by using herbs, and those who wished to gain more knowledge to help in healing others. The hundreds of members became thousands, and Mrs Leyel wrote many books that have become reference works for those studying natural medicine.

Another herbalist with a world-wide reputation is Juliette de Baïracli Levy, an Israeli lady who has spent a large part of her life living amongst some of the primitive peoples in so-called "under-developed" countries, learning from them their herbal lore and usage. The American Indians, the natives of several South American countries, and the gipsies all over the world, have given her a wealth of information on how they manage to raise their families and their live-stock under extremely poor conditions. In many cases, their health and vigour, even in old age, should bring shame on our affluent, enlightened society, with its increasing toll from asthma and obesity and early coronaries. Two of her books are listed in the bibliography at the end of this book, and I can recommend them to those wishing to raise livestock by natural methods or to care for the health and well-being of the family without recourse to unnatural products.

In conclusion, let me tell you some interesting recent developments in America. Once the loudest advocates of the "miracle" laboratory-produced drugs, American chemical and drug companies have had in the last few years an astonishing change of heart. In *Popular Mechanics* (April 1960) an article titled "In Search of Plants that Cure" (James Joseph) revealed that these same drug companies are spending many of their millions in searching out once again plants that have the reputation of healing or curing disease all over the world. Parties of chemists and botanists are being sent out to such out-of-the-way places as Iceland and Yucatan with instructions to bring back any plants known locally as of medicinal use. One researcher (Dr Alfred Taylor of the University of Texas) says, "We've never had as much success with chemicals invented by man as we're having with plant extracts." How many "witches" were burnt at the stake in medieval times for saying the same? And how many herb users in health and sickness today are figures of fun to their neighbours and long-suffering friends? Perhaps pharmaceutical companies are the ones who have taken the wrong turning for many years.

The millions spent in money and time by such firms, and the advertising they will undoubtedly use, may once again make it seem important to grow the physic gardens of long ago. The wheel is turning full circle, and the "green revolution" appears to be not very far away. I hope the following chapters will give you some of the necessary ammunition to be in the vanguard.

General Information
on Growing Herbs

In answering questions put to me by those wishing to grow
herbs in their garden, I have found the commonest problems
come under the headings below:

Where is it best to grow herbs?

What special conditions do they require?

How can herbs best be raised from seed?

How else can I propagate them?

What are the best herbs to grow, and how can I use them:

How are fresh herbs different from the dried ones, and how
can I dry my own?

Can herbs be grown indoors?

What is the best way to control insect pests and disease:

Each of these questions has a different answer, depending on
your soil and climatic conditions and the seasonal conditions in
your part of the world. So I have tried to make the information
as general as possible, leaving some adjustment to be made to
your own particular circumstances.

Where Is It Best to Grow Herbs

"Where to grow" of course depends entirely on the size and
type of your garden, and whether you wish to grow the plants
for horticultural interest or for health or culinary use.

My own garden has herbs in the most unlikely places—
under the rose bushes, spreading wild in my gravel driveway
and creeping right up to the bricks of the barbecue where they
get singed every so often. Let me hasten to say (lest you think
I'm a "plant and pray" gardener) that they also grow in a
series of formal circular beds, some with brick stepping-stones
so I can move easily amongst them; many more in a long,

thin, crescent-shaped bed; and a few, especially the mints, confined to large containers (14- to 18-inch pots or tubs). I have in my kitchen courtyard a strawberry pot with some culinary standbys, marjoram, sage, lemon-scented and garden thyme, and a small basil; and on a wide sunny shelf in my laundry I have most of the year small punnets or seed-boxes with young seedlings or newly sown seeds, or some quick-growing mustard and cress sprouts for salads.

So the questions seems best answered "Herbs will grow wherever you want them to!" But the plants have their individual likes and dislikes, as set out in the chapters on each particular herb, and it would be best to find out what these are before choosing plants for a special place in your garden.

Here are a few suggestions for formal beds.

THE LADDER. This should be a long rectangular bed with narrow pathways across for "rungs", to enable you to tend and pick the plants. This pattern is best used for small-growing herbs such as marjoram, oregano, salad burnet, winter savory and all the varieties of thyme. It is also best if planted only with perennial evergreen herbs, so your "ladder" does not have a step missing for several months of the year.

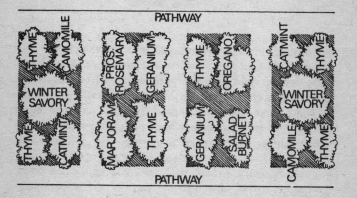

THE WHEEL. In the nineteenth century herbs were often grown decoratively inside the spokes of an old cartwheel laid flat on the ground. The hub of the wheel raised the rim slightly above ground level, providing a low supporting "fence" as well as a border to the garden. Old cartwheels cannot now be picked up on the side of any busy road as they could be then, and you can't really grow herbs decoratively surrounded by a defunct inner tube. So, to compromise, try the next category.

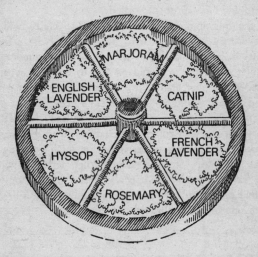

THE CIRCLE. This is my favourite shape for growing herbs. The ancients (and Carl Jung), attributed a protective value to the perfect circle, and I have always found my herbs grow most happily in a circular bed. In the centre section, place tall-growing plants such as lemongrass, French lavender or bush rosemary. Then plant another circle outside the inner row of stepping stones, with the medium growers — English lavender, lemon balm, lemon or rose-scented geraniums, marjoram, prostrate rosemary. Around the outside edge of the bed, plant the ground-covers, all the thyme varieties, a few camomile roots, several clumps of garlic and onion chives, and some pennyroyal on the shadiest side, where it will have some shelter from the taller plants.

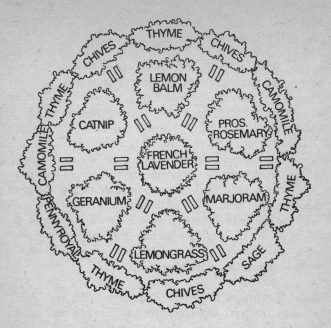

Now you will have after one season a garden centrepiece that will surprise you with its decorative potential. It has always amazed me that more herbs are not grown for their good looks as well as their usefulness and their perfume and flavour. Some are very showy indeed, and deserve a place in the herbaceous border as well as the utility garden. Chicory (if allowed to flower), the brilliant pink yarrow, santolina with its ferny, feathery, grey foliage and yellow-orange flower heads, and my old friend, tansy, with its 3-foot-high bright green fronds and yellow button flowers, are all worth while. Be a bit wary of putting tansy in the flower garden, though, otherwise you will have a border full of this vigorously growing herb before many seasons have passed. But for that corner where "nothing will grow", plant tansy and stand back.

If possible, avoid planting herbs near the roots of trees. They do not like competing with the voracious roots for the available food, and will grow tall, thin and straggly. Save them a spot in the open garden instead.

Many herbs will grow in the warmth of a rockery or rock garden. But make sure there is sufficient depth of soil in each pocket to give their strong root systems room to forage. One friend who had difficulty with insufficient soil in the pockets complained to me, "I have a lovely rock garden, but it grows nothing but lovely rocks!" I would not advise planting in a rockery any of the herbs required for their roots: you may have to dismantle the whole shebang to harvest the crop. When setting out the plants in a rockery, it is advisable to give them a great deal of water for the first few weeks to minimize the baking effect of the hot sun on the rocks.

So the choice of "where to grow" is really up to you. Be inventive; design a herb garden best suited to your own herb needs; and you will have the satisfaction of being architect as well as engineer and chief labourer.

What Conditions Do Herbs Require?

SUNSHINE AND WELL-WORKED LIGHT SOIL. The first requirement for most herbs is sunshine. The next most important requirement is the fertility and physical consistency of the soil. A whole chapter is given later in this book to soil preparation and composting, but in this chapter I shall discuss two aspects only: the soil *must* be well-drained, and it must have the essential nutriment needed by any plant for healthy vigorous growth.

The drainage can be easily dealt with (on paper anyway!). Digging a trench and laying crocks or gravel or agricultural drainage pipes or channels sounds like, and is, hard work; but no herb will grow with constant "wet feet". In places where sandy or light shale soils predominate, drainage is not such a severe problem; but don't think you can get away with growing herbs in heavy soils which, after rain, are waterlogged for days. Sage is one of the first to succumb, then the leaves start to yellow on the thymes, and before long some very sick herb plants are all that remain. The time spent in initial drainage of the site is well worth it.

18

Some herb growers prefer to put their plants in raised beds to meet this drainage requirement. A low double stone or brick wall, the hollow filled with rich soil, and sufficient water available, is a happy hunting-ground for all the hardiest sun-lovers. Try prostrate rosemary, Westmoreland or caraway thyme, bush basil in the spring, and a few plants of marjoram or sage, and watch them revel in these conditions.

FEEDING. Food for the young plants is best put into the soil before they are set out, particularly with a perennial bed, which will not be disturbed again for several years. I have found the only fertilizers to use are the natural organic manures and compost. (See chapter on soil fertility.) All my own herbs are organically grown, with no chemical or synthetic fertilizers and no dangerous sprays, so their feeding is completely natural and their flavour and aroma unchanged.

Blood and bone, in my opinion, is still the best concentrated food to be deeply dug into the soil when preparing the bed, for its nutriment is released more slowly, and is available to the plants over a longer period. Dig down or break up the soil to a depth of 18 inches or 2 feet if possible. It will repay you in allowing strong, free-ranging root systems to penetrate the soil freely. Into this loosened bed dig blood and bone at the rate of about 5 pounds to a circular bed 12 to 15 feet in diameter. A smaller bed should have about 4 or 5 handfuls per square yard well dug into the loosened top 8 to 12 inches of soil. This is fairly heavy feeding, and if your soil is rich and full of humus already, less blood and bone will suffice. *Do not overfeed:* this is the worst possible treatment for herbs. You will have abundant growth, yes, but less flavour and aroma, more susceptibility to insect pests and diseases, and in many cases no flowering at all. The best herb plants for any use whatsoever are those with good basic feeding to start with. Then do not disturb them, but let their flavour and oil content mature slowly as they grow. The most flavourful thymes and marjoram are the little woody plants, not the leggy, overfed giants which the caterpillars will love as much as you do.

When the plants are set out, spread a layer of coarse compost

19

material (peat-moss will pinch-hit for compost if you don't have a bin ready) and fork it loosely into the top few inches of soil. This will stop the soil caking and crusting when watered, and will give the roots near the surface some loose material in which to spread.

If possible, give herbs only natural foods, and avoid the instant dissolvable fertilizers: they tend to upset the powerful little mineral and vitamin factories of the herb plants themselves, and can even be fatal. Regular dressings of organic compost, forked lightly into the top-soil, duplicate the natural conditions under which all the plants grow best.

LIME. Nearly all the commonly-grown herbs need an alkaline soil. For soils that tend to be acid and are somewhat deficient in magnesium, dolomite, a natural mixture of magnesium carbonate and calcium carbonate, is preferable to lime (calcium carbonate only), to give the necessary alkalinity. A sure-fire test for soil acidity is this: If your garden grows camellias, azaleas and rhododendrons to perfection, or if it grows in its natural state a fine array of bush plants, it will need lime or dolomite added to the section where you wish to plant herbs.

A light scattering of dolomite can be put through the loose topsoil before planting, *together with* any manures or blood and bone. This is contrary to accepted gardening practice, but was recommended to me by the Department of Agriculture in New South Wales. Their booklet, *Building up Fertility in the Garden*, is invaluable. No doubt the Agriculture Departments in other states and countries will have similar material available.

WATERING. Herbs must have regular water for their best growth (in conjunction with the good drainage mentioned previously), even though many of them can still thrive in dry conditions. Water seems to be necessary for the production of a high oil content.

The herbs can all be watered even in the heat of a bright summer's day, particularly basil, whose brittle leaves and stems need moisture when the sun is at its hottest. In cooler weather it is advisable to water them in mid-morning so the soil will not be too damp and cold overnight.

So now your herbs are ready to set out in their permanent positions. Keep a section for annuals, another separate one for perennials, or if planting them amongst the flower beds and shrubs remember their individual likes and dislikes and they will give you beauty and usefulness from season to season.

How Can Herbs Best Be Raised from Seed?

Almost all the common herbs can be easily raised from seed, some notable exceptions being French tarragon, which very rarely sets seed and must be propagated from root or stem cuttings, and lemongrass, one of the rush family, whose clumps must be broken apart with the spade and offsets planted.

I have always found it best to start the seeds in punnets or seed boxes rather than the open garden: conditions can be better controlled and losses due to sudden climatic changes can be minimized. Even seedlings that do not transplant with great ease can be handled with extra care and gentleness and coaxed into settling into their eventual places outdoors.

Use up your old margarine cartons or ice-cream trays, punch a dozen or so holes around the outside edge of the bottom, fill to 1 inch from the top with a mixture of $\frac{1}{3}$ sand, $\frac{1}{3}$ good loam and $\frac{1}{3}$ peat-moss, and add a sprinkle of lime to the mixture. Sow the seed thinly and cover with a light layer of the same mixture, then gently firm down with a piece of flat board (or a matchbox will do for a punnet). Soak well with water from one of those laundry sprinkler bottles, cover loosely with a piece of clear plastic with holes punched every few inches, and in the warmer weather 4 to 10 days should see the seed leaves showing through. (See the chapters on individual herbs for some notable exceptions to this germination period.) It is wise to familiarize yourself with the approximate germination period of all the herbs described. This will save you many anxious trips to the laundry searching for seedlings that are not due to break through for another fortnight. There must be millions of seeds of parsley that have germinated in the garbage bin or the rubbish heap because they did not show through in a week. (Parsley can take up to eight weeks before you see any green shoots piercing the soil.)

Keep the trays or boxes moist, and remove the plastic each night, taking it off altogether as soon as the shoots break through. A shelf in the laundry is ideal for raising seeds: you see it almost every day and the generally moist atmosphere helps with germination.

The first two leaves to show through, the seed leaves, are necessary for the nourishment of the growing seed and the new plant, so do not disturb the punnet until the next pair of true leaves is growing strongly. Then put the punnets outside in a sheltered but warm position, and just watch those herbs race away. They can be set out into the open garden at any time after this hardening period, usually about a week to a fortnight. Plant them in the late afternoon in soil that has been well-watered during the day, dribble further water around the base of each plant (not on the leaves), and the next morning they will be ready to start the day with the most amazing release of perfume. I have noted this phenomenon time and time again. The plants seem to be so thankful to be out in the sunshine and open soil that a sudden burst of fragrance is their "thank you". This happens most noticeably with the setting out of relatively mature plants from pots into the open garden. So be sure to walk round your garden the next day and enjoy this promise of things to come.

Herbs contain all the essentials of their flavour and aroma right from the tiny seedling stage, and if you forget to label them or the label has washed off, bruise one of the tiny leaves and taste and smell it, and you should be able to identify the plant.

Never leave the plastic covering over the seed boxes all the time, for fungus and mould may grow in the damp soil. The purists will want to sterilize the seed-box soil first by putting it in a baking dish in a warm oven for about 20 minutes, or running hot water through the soil to kill the spores: but with ordinary care this should not be necessary. Watering with camomile tea (See Camomile) will stop "damping off".

Always buy your herb seeds from a reputable source. Most seed merchants are now carrying stocks, but beware of those dusty sun-bleached packets on the back shelf in the hardware store. Your nursery is the best bet. Their turnover is high, ensuring that the seed is always the freshest available, their suppliers are reliable, and their reputation is at stake.

How Else Can I Propagate Them?

Many herbs growing low to the ground propagate and increase by natural "layering". This happens when a stem lying along the ground sends out roots into the soil from the point where it touches. If you want more plants than those natural "layers", help the process along by selecting long bendable stems and pinning them down at one or two points with a hair-pin as shown below. Water well to encourage root growth down into the soil at the point of contact. After several weeks, a whole new plant will be forming, and you can sever it from the parent plant after about six weeks, and move it to its new location.

This is an ideal way to increase your herb plants, as it involves very little work or supervision, and does not disturb the parent plant which can still flourish in the same spot with no set-back to its growth.

Suitable herbs for layering are lemon balm, catmint, the scented geraniums, horehound, hyssop, marjoram, the mints, rosemary (slower to root), sage, savory, and all the thymes.

PROSTRATE ROSEMARY

Many herbs grow well from cuttings, too. Take them in the post-flowering period if possible, or if you are not letting your herbs flower (in order to get the best fragrance and flavour), take cuttings after the new growth of the spring has hardened off a bit, otherwise they may wilt and not strike. Late summer is often best of all, as the stems are now strong and more woody, and cuttings taken with a "heel" of old wood at the base have every chance of striking.

I prefer to use the same seed-box soil mixture for striking cuttings. I have found that the sand medium often recommended is not so satisfactory for herbs, and the added nutriment in the richer mixture has no harmful effect on tender new herb roots. In fact, cuttings strike so well that they then suffer very little acclimatization worries when transferred to similar soil in the open garden, window box or pot. Put the cuttings fairly close together round the outside edge of a large terracotta pot, and water them sufficiently to keep the soil moist. A mist-sprayer or small atomizer is useful, too, to keep the foliage damp during the day. Each time you pass the cutting pot, have the spray handy, as tests have proved that cuttings root better if their foliage is kept slightly moist.

You can tell when your cuttings have rooted and are strong enough to transplant by observing their leaf growth. You will have stripped most of the old leaves off when first planting them, and perhaps nipped off the top shoot as well. When new leaves are growing strongly, you can be sure your cutting is alive. Leave it a week or two longer, then transplant to its new home. Unless these new leaves are formed, the cutting has not taken root, and is not viable.

Almost all herbs grow well from cuttings, with the exception of clump-forming ones like borage, comfrey, dandelion, lemongrass and horseradish.

In What Ways Can Fresh Herbs Be Used, and What Is the Best Selection to Grow?
The traditional uses of herbs in cooking, and in toilet and

medicinal preparations, would fill a much larger book than this one.

By all means, always serve your oily fish with fennel and your pizza with fresh oregano, but *be inventive* as well. Some of the culinary masterpieces of French and Continental cuisine came about because the cook was out of mushrooms and used truffles instead; or the mint was dormant for the winter, so the lamb had to be flavoured with rosemary. Try some new combinations.

All the culinary herbs are quite beneficial in the quantities generally used to make herb teas or to garnish or flavour food, so let your imagination blossom, and try some hot herb slaw (page 143) or herbal variations on an omelette, and take it from there.

Remember to use only a *small* quantity of the fresh herb to flavour a dish. One sprig of sweet basil with two or three leaves on a stem 2 inches long will be enough to flavour a whole salad bowl; or chop one or two leaves and sprinkle over fresh tomatoes. One of our family favourites is onions and tomatoes cooked quickly together in a little butter, served on wholemeal toast with several chopped leaves of basil sprinkled over the top before serving, or a little sprig of marjoram or oregano added to the hot butter for several seconds before adding the vegetables.

Herb oils and vinegars can be made quite easily at home. Both make excellent gifts and can dress up an everyday meal to make it a "speciality of the house".

Buy a good white wine vinegar. This is essential, as inferior quality will not give the herb flavours a chance. Then find some leftover bottles in decorative shapes, preferably with a screwtop (corks tend to take up the herb flavour). Pick a handful of your favourite savoury herb at its best, bruise it well with the mortar and pestle, and add to each handful about a pint of the vinegar, then bottle and seal well. Leave for one week, then strain. Repeat the process with another handful of the fresh herb if a stronger flavour is required. After the second week, strain to remove all leaves and stems, and return to the bottle,

25

sealing well. Then use the vinegar in salad dressings to give that magic *je ne sais quoi* that will keep your guests guessing. Tarragon, savory, basil, marjoram and sage are a few suitable herbs.

Herb oils have many uses. They can be used in salad dressings, and a few drops added to cooking oil when quickly frying vegetables or meat can transform the dish completely. I do not eat sausages, but a friend who does tells me that a few drops of rosemary oil, added when frying them, turns the humble "snag" into a connoisseur's delight. Here is how to make a herb oil:

Buy some good quality bland oil, like safflower or almond (peanut and olive oil are not suitable) and fill a screwtopped jar ⅔ full with it. Then pick a good handful of the herb you need, it may be rosemary, thyme, lavender, or peppermint, and bruise it well in the mortar and pestle, adding a little white wine vinegar as you go (about 1 tablespoon). Then add the crushed herb and vinegar to the jar containing the oil, seal tightly, and shake it vigorously. Stand the jar on a hot sunny window-ledge or against a wall where it will get maximum heat. This is best done in the hot summer months, but if you want to do it in winter, stand it in the *warm* (not hot) zone of a radiator, oil heater or fire. Shake it well every day for about three weeks. Test the oil by rubbing it on your skin. If the fragrance is still there after a few minutes, the oil is "done". If not, crush some more of the herb and repeat for another couple of weeks. Then strain, and bottle, sealing well.

When you get that tense, headachy tiredness after a stressful day, rub a little rosemary oil gently into your temples; it soothes and relaxes. Peppermint oil is good for all muscular tiredness. Lavender oil is gentle and relaxing to painful rheumatic joints; and thyme oil, the most powerful of all, can relieve migraine headaches caused by tension and overstrain.

Many recipes and instructions for simple aids to health and relief in illness have been included in the chapters on each individual herb. In general, don't attempt to diagnose the illnesses of your family, your neighbours and your friends and prescribe herbs for them until you have either a comprehensive knowledge of natural medicine or a good solicitor or both! Orthodox medicine and the law still frown on unqualified or unskilled practitioners. Any natureopathic physician can help you with diagnostic problems, and then you can with his advice include in your diet the herbs that can be beneficial in your particular case.

No one, of course, can be stopped from dosing *himself*; and, as you learn about herbs and their uses, you can make herb teas or simple medicinal preparations with the fresh leaves and dried roots from your own garden. Never take more than the suggested quantities. Most herbs have a powerful immediate action within the body, and increased quantities will not mean speedier relief. Nature works slowly to remove not the *symptoms* of disease but the *cause* of it. It's no use trying to stop the sneezing misery of hay fever or chronic asthmatic troubles by treating the mucous membranes of the respiratory system if the cause of the disease is faulty kidney action, or some vitamin or mineral deficiency. It may also take the body a long time to throw off the cumulative effects of drugs built up over a long period. So don't be impatient at the apparent slowness of natural treatment. Your satisfaction will be the greater in the end if you get rid of the *cause* and therefore of any symptoms.

My own son, who for several years had chronic hay-fever that did not respond to orthodox medical treatment, lost it completely in three months after natural herbal treatment of the *cause*. He has never had an attack since.

Of course, you must first want to be healthy. So many people now seem, in that lovely Victorian phrase, to "enjoy ill health", literally. It becomes an acceptable excuse for dodging life's problems. If you really want to enjoy *good* health, it is up to you to do something about it.

Diet is a very important factor in maintaining health or correcting illness. Give your body its natural food: whole grains, salads, fruit, meat in moderation (if you cannot give it up altogether), wholemeal bread and flour, and all those concentrated energy goodies like dates, figs, nuts, and dried fruits. You will lose weight, and your energy and enjoyment of life will grow each day. Have a browse around your local health food store and see what a tempting array of exotic, tasty, nourishing food comes under the heading of "what is good for you". You will be astonished at the variety of gourmet meals you can prepare from natural ingredients.

I have known many, many people who have been dissatisfied with the results obtained from orthodox medicine and have turned as a last resort to a natureopath or herbalist. I have never yet met *one* who has been dissatisfied with natural medicine and natural living and returned to his former diet and chemical drugs.

Now for some advice on selecting which herbs to grow. Most people want to start with, say, half a dozen. All depends on your own taste and requirements. If you eat a salad every day, you will want such herbs as chicory, dandelion, parsley, chives, perhaps Florence fennel (the bulbous root section is used), and basil. If your taste runs to hot savoury casseroles or vegetable and egg dishes, choose some of the culinary herbs like marjoram, sage, thyme, dill, chervil, and winter savory. For cool drinks and fruit cups try salad burnet, borage and all the mints; and for herb teas, some of the best are camomile, peppermint and spearmint, comfrey, lemongrass and sage. For the keen gardener, yarrow, comfrey, valerian, tansy, rue, southernwood—all are valuable as described in their individual chapters; while a selection of the medicinal herbs I would never be without are chives (or garlic), lemon balm, comfrey, horehound, horseradish, hyssop, rosemary, sage, thyme and yarrow.

Whichever category you wish to choose from, learn as much as you can about each herb so you can use and enjoy it to the full. This book contains only some forty-odd herbs. Many thousands of plants can be classed as herbs, with characteristics beneficial to man. Another book is already in preparation, extending the list to such plants as nasturtium, calendula, burdock, coltsfoot, Golden Rod, equisetum, and many more. The list is endless.

How Are Fresh Herbs Different from Dried Ones, and How Can They Best Be Dried?

Fresh herbs can be used wherever dry herbs are called for in a recipe, and in most cases the flavour is vastly superior. Drying any plant removes a lot of its vitality, oils and vitamins; but if you wish to use chives in mid-winter, you must either dry or freeze the fresh herbs to maintain a continuous supply.

Very high quality dried herbs are now packaged in Australia. One firm is Somerset Cottage, the family business of Rosemary Hemphill, the author of *Spice and Savour* and *Fragrance and Flavour*. In general, when dried herbs are called for in a recipe and you wish to substitute fresh herbs, use *3 times* the quantity listed.

You can dry your own herbs in many different ways. The best and easiest way for the home gardener is to lay out the fresh-cut leaves or flowers on screens made by stretching those left-over ends of nylon net or terylene curtaining (or even clean hessian) over one or two old picture-frames. Tack the material around the outer edge, and put the frames where air can circulate under as well as over the drying herbs. A *dry* shelf in the laundry (if it's not too sunny), or in a storeroom, or even on top of that old cupboard in the garage (not where your car exhaust fumes are going to hit the tray), are all good places to dry the herbs. Never dry them in the sun; you will lose almost all their goodness.

You can also dry herbs tied in small bunches hung head downwards from tacks along the edge of a shelf, or from brackets, or underneath overhead cupboards in your kitchen. I often have bunches of lavender or the scented geraniums drying like this hung from the black iron brackets of my herb shelf in the kitchen. This way you can get some of the perfume while they are drying. Never hang them in a spot where steam or condensation will get to them.

Pick healthy fresh leaves, or flowers when they are just open, after the morning dew has evaporated and they are quite dry. Spread these carefully in a thin layer on your screens, turn them every few days until they are crisp and crackly. Then rub the leaves from the stalks, bottle them in *glass screw-topped jars* (never in plastic or brown paper bags), and seal tightly. Write the date and the name somewhere on each jar, and if you haven't used up the herbs in twelve months' time, tip them out onto the compost heap or around your herb plants. Dried herbs have a limited shelf life under these conditions, so give the compost heap the benefit of their natural material, and put up another batch for yourself.

If moisture is visible several days after bottling, tip the leaves out for further drying. I always like to let the weather work for me here, and quickly rush out and harvest when we have those hot, drying winds that last for three or four days. In such conditions you can bottle the herbs with confidence in five or six days, sometimes less. Never attempt to dry herbs in humid weather—the results will always be poor and the drying time so long that most of the goodness will be gone.

The roots of some herbs are also dried, like horseradish, comfrey, valerian and dandelion. These need different treatment. Dig the roots at the time recommended in the chapters on individual herbs. Wash and scrub them and cut off any fibrous or hair roots. Then cut the root lengthwise in slivers about ¼ inch wide, and these can be dried either on the screens (this takes much longer) or in a warm oven with the door slightly ajar. An eagle eye must be kept on them in the latter case, and be prepared for some failures until experience teaches you. The test for dryness is that a sliver of the root will crack and break when bent. If it is not dry, it will still be pliable and will only bend. Store the dried roots in a glass jar lined with tissue paper until you need them. Then grate the required quantity.

Herbs can also be frozen to preserve them through the winter months. Some, like chives, suit this process very well, as does parsley. Snip off the fresh, perfect leaves, wash them and chop them well and immediately put them in tiny foil envelopes into the freezer. Only put in one envelope what you will need for each dish, and keep the different varieties separate.

Be sure to label each envelope clearly, or you may find basil in the soup or savory in the apple pie!

POT-POURRI. Dried herbs and spices are used in the making of pot-pourri, the scented mixture of flowers, leaves, roots and aromatic spices used in those little pottery jars, and bags or sachets. Believe it or not, the name comes from the French *pourrir*, to rot, and is derived from the original method of manufacture, semi-dried material being mixed with oils and perfumed waters and allowed literally to rot. The resulting sticky mess *had* to be put into opaque containers. But the perfume, using salt and orris root, benzoin gum, and various other preservatives, was delightful.

Nowadays, the most popular way to make pot-pourri is by the dry method. Dry some of the following; lemon balm, lemongrass, rose petals (the old scented "cabbage roses" are the best), lavender heads, violet petals, white jasmine, a small quantity of lemon or garden thyme, rosemary, orange and lemon blossom or dried orange or lemon peel, and leaves of the scented geraniums (rose and lemon are the best). Dry all these thoroughly separately, then mix together in a large container, together with a very small quantity of cinnamon, several blades of mace, or a few cloves if you wish.

Now pack a layer about 1 inch deep in the bottom of a half-gallon glass jar (a smaller glass jar will do for a smaller quantity), and sprinkle with a mixture of half salt and half powdered orris root. Fill up the jar this way with alternate layers, pressing it down tightly as you go, then seal well. (Orris root, by the way, is the rhizome of *Iris germanica* or *Iris florentina*, the common purple, mauve or white garden iris. It can be bought from herb stockists, but you can make your own by drying the roots as described here previously, and rubbing them through a fine grater or pulverizing them in a blender. They have no perfume when fresh, only when dried.)

Leave your jar now for one month. Then unpack, stir all around, and fill small pottery jars, decorative containers, or small dainty bags of silk or taffeta. This dry mix is ideally suited for making sachet bags for clothing cupboards and linen

31

drawers, or for scenting a box of writing paper. Remember to stir the pot or rub the sachet occasionally: herbs release their perfume only when bruised.

Can Herbs be Grown Indoors?

Quite a few of the herbs mentioned in this book will grow well indoors (chervil, indeed grows somewhat better inside than out), but herbs grown this way should all have light or reflected sunlight or warmth on them for at least a part of each day.

During the autumn, choose several of the smaller plants from your nursery, like basil, marjoram or a young rosemary. It is best to repot them into a larger container to promote initial growth, and then stand them in a sunny corner of your kitchen or near a window. They will also grow well in a covered patio corner or enclosed sunroom, provided they get water periodically. Late summer and early autumn sowing of basil will produce young plants ready to pot out and carry you through the winter, but only if you can grow them indoors in a warm atmosphere. Basil is a frost-tender plant, and the first icy fingers will scorch and blacken it.

Herbs grown in pots indoors will remain more dwarfed than outdoor plants. But their flavour and perfume will be almost as good as if grown outside.

Window boxes are a pleasant way to grow herbs indoors. If you live in an old house with wide window-sills, get someone to make you a shallow metal tray about 1½ inches deep, put in it a layer of gravel, crocks or decorative small stones, and stand your pots on top. You can water them freely and still have good drainage. A true window box made of waterproof ply and painted white looks very Mediterranean and is utilitarian as well. Suspend it with plugs into the bricks, or on chains as shown; but remember it will be fairly weighty filled with wet soil, so make your fastenings strong and secure.

Bore ⅜-inch drainage holes spaced 5 to 8 inches apart in the bottom of the box, then put a layer of broken terracotta crocks or gravel in the bottom. Fill up with the usual potting

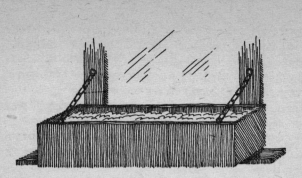

mixture of ⅓ coarse sand, ⅓ loam and ⅓ peat moss and compost; and in this case some blood and bone and a sprinkling of dolomite can be added as well, together with some pieces of charcoal, if available, to keep the soil sweet. Just a sprinkling of the blood and bone will do, but mix it thoroughly through, and leave the whole box for several days before putting in your plants. Just tease out the roots slightly when you up-end the nursery pot, or dip the plant briefly in *warm* water to free the outside roots.

Pick the sunniest window sill, and hope it is your kitchen or dining room, then you can snip off fresh leaves for your salad mixed at the table.

Good plants for a window box are marjoram, thyme, basil, chervil (in the cooler months only, as it needs some shade in the summer), chives and parsley.

Pots can also be kept in one of those planter stands with metal rings to take each pot, but watering with this type of installation can be a problem.

Terra-cotta pots, or decorative ceramic containers, with their own saucers underneath, are still the happiest accommodation for plants indoors. The plants can breathe through the pot, and are less subject to overwatering problems. The best way to water is to lift the pot and test the weight. A very heavy pot means there is enough water, a lightweight one means water is needed. Give water until it starts to trickle into the saucer below. Let the plant stand for an hour, then tip out any surplus water in the saucer. Don't on any account let herb pots sit in a saucer of water for any length of time. Their "wet feet" may bring on a chill from which they will not recover.

Try some of the peppermint or rose-scented geraniums indoors too, and brush against them every so often to release their perfume.

For pots, use the same potting mixture as for the window-box, and once again allow it to stand for several days before planting, so the blood and bone will not harm the tender roots.

Indoor herb plants are certainly worth growing if you want fresh herbs in the winter as well. If possible, leave the plants indoors one season only, then give them a spell in the open garden.

Don't try to grow the tall herbs like lovage, chicory or tansy indoors, nor the deep-rooted ones like horseradish, comfrey or angelica. They do not like to be confined, and grow much better out in the elements.

How Can Insect Pests and Diseases Be Controlled?

This is the 64-dollar question for all herb growers. The very edible nature of herbs means that any methods used to combat insect pests or disease must be carefully chosen to ensure that they are of a non-cumulative, non-toxic nature. No gardener or cook would voluntarily poison the family foodstuffs, and yet we are asked to do this by some manufacturers of the many chemicals and sprays at present advertised. Where there is any doubt at all as to the possible dangers of eating food thus contaminated, it would be wise to use only natural products harmless to humans; so some careful sorting-out of the "good-ies" and "baddies" on the nurseryman's insecticide shelves must be undertaken. Pay special attention to the time that must elapse before plants sprayed with anything at all can be eaten. This is printed on the pack by all reputable firms.

I have read every publication I can lay my hands on in this regard, and have talked to gardeners, to Department of Agriculture authorities, and to workers in the chemical spray industry. From their freely given information, and my own experience, have come several pesticides of natural vegetable origin that I can recommend as having been used with safety over and over again.

The Bio-dynamic Gardening Association in America, and the Henry Doubleday Research Association in Essex, England, have several publications relating to insect control that make interesting reading for gardeners who wish to use natural products only on edible crops.

The main pests attacking herbs are very few: Grasshoppers, the large bright green variety as well as the speckled brown, dearly love some of the more succulent herbs like comfrey, catnip, and lemon balm, especially if the weather is humid; caterpillars, particularly the green "loopy" type, can strip young plants of tarragon, lemon and garden thyme and basil, and the young leaves of salad burnet and marjoram, unless a close watch is kept; and the slugs and snails roll up in numbers each night at the prospect of fresh horseradish leaves for supper. These, however, seem to be the limit of the insect pests, with the exception of a few aphis which sometimes colonize on the fennel or dill stems below the flowers. The general health of the plants, the state of the soil in which they grow, and the natural food given to them, all help to protect them when insects and snails are about. A well-cared-for garden will have fewer insect pests than a neglected one.

When you think of all the pests that menace garden flowers and vegetables, the score for herbs is very low, perhaps owing to the potency of their aromatic oils, many of which insects of all descriptions cannot stand. So great is their dislike for garlic chives, tansy, rue, lavender, santolina, that they will never come near them; so these herbs together can be made into a very powerful insecticide. Wormwood and southernwood are other pungent herbs which no predator will eat or destroy, because of the strong smell of ether given off from their foliage.

So in this way these herbs can help keep the rest of the garden free of pests if planted amongst the flowers and shrubs, and if bruised gently to free their aromatic oils. One large rose nursery now sells plants of garlic chives with each rose order, to keep the aphis away and increase the perfume of the roses. It really works!

If you have only a small herb patch, insects are best removed by hand. This does not involve much time or trouble, and you know then you have herbs in perfect condition for the table or the hot "brew". However, if you cannot keep an eye on the plants each day, you may prefer to spray or dust them with several of the following:

Derris dust is a pure organic powder made from the derris root. It kills on contact caterpillars and grasshoppers, but is even more effective when mixed with pyrethrum (*Pyrethrum cinerariafolium*), the South African plant which now figures largely in many proprietary insect sprays. Incidentally, this plant is not the ordinary white garden Pyrethrum Daisy, which has no effect on insects at all. If you can obtain both of these unadulterated by chemical additives, you can spray or dust your herbs just before dusk, and have them safe by morning, ensuring that the bees will not be driven away or killed too. Both these preparations have been extensively tested and found to be safe for human or animal consumption, provided the recommended instructions as to the amount to be used are followed.

Rhubarb leaves (which you know must never be eaten) are deadly poisonous to aphis and most sucking insects. Make up a batch as follows: Cut up 3 pounds of the leaves, and boil in 3 quarts of water for 30 minutes, then strain, and add 4 ounces of a soft soap (that common laundry variety is best), and dissolve it well. This spray when cool can be used to kill aphis on roses, but if you use it on herbs, remember to leave the plants for at least a fortnight before cutting them for the table.

Tobacco dust is another good organic insecticide, but can be hard to come by now. I have even offered to sweep up the floor at one of the large cigarette-packaging companies, but, as you can imagine, I was laughed off the premises. Any of you who live in a tobacco-growing district may be able to get the left-overs from the drying-shed floors. These can be prepared as follows: Boil 4 ounces of tobacco dust (cigarette ends will do if you are a smoker, but remove the filter tips), in a gallon of water for 30 minutes. Strain the clear brown liquid, and bottle it *carefully labelled* and away from small children, if not using it at once. It is quite poisonous, so care must be taken; but it quickly breaks down in the soil some two or three weeks after spraying, and it is safe to eat any leaves after this period.

Chemical insecticide manufacturers are beginning to recognize the increasing demand for "safe" sprays. As this book is written, two are on the market advertised as "bio-degradable", and safe for edible crops.

Herbs seldom suffer from fungus diseases if the soil is properly drained and adequately limed (or dolomited) and sufficient organic compost is put into the ground, in which live the "helpers" as well as the predators. Many types of micro-organisms found in natural compost kill off the mildew and fungus-producing spores living in poor soil. Lime or dolomite is necessary in the soil not only as a direct plant *food* (I say that with the backing of an agronomist in high places), but also to kill off many of the disease-producing elements. I have grown sage plants under controlled conditions, one section with dolomite in the container and one without. During the very wet summer that ensued, the dolomited plants sailed through unscathed, while the others dropped their yellowed leaves and eventually succumbed completely to root-rot.

If you do suspect a plant of having a fungous or root disease, one effective ground spray is the following: Obtain if you can the leaves of *Equisetum arvense*, Horsetail, or Mare's Tail, from your nursery, or the dried leaves through your natureopathic physician. Boil 1 part equisetum to 50 parts of water for 15 to 20 minutes. Do not make the solution any stronger, as the herb is a very potent one. Water this around the base of the affected plants (not on the foliage) on soil which has been soaked well the previous day. Equisetum has a very high silica content.

37

Another remedy for a sickly plant, where root disease is suspected, was given to me by a very knowledgeable "herb lady". Make a circle of copper wire (fairly thick gauge, or several strands of thinner gauge) and place it round the base of the ailing plant and about ¼-inch under the soil. This is a simple remedy for one frequent cause of plant ill-health—a copper deficiency in the soil, reducing the plant's normal resistance to disease. My favourite "perfect circle" may also have a lot to do with the protection and increased vigour given to the plant.

So, since many herbs are natural insect repellents, grow them beside other herbs which tend to be much less lucky. The chapters on each herb will give you more specific information, but here is a list of herbs that pests will seldom if ever attack: garlic chives, scented geraniums, lavender, parsley, pennyroyal, rue, santolina and tansy (except for an odd snail or two).

Use some of your herbs to free your kitchen of ants, too. Dried tansy leaves, rubbed to release their oils, will keep ants away from honey or sugar, or will drive them away even after they are already infesting a cupboard. Just rub some of the leaves between your fingers to release their oils, and sprinkle a small handful around on your cupboard shelves. A pot of basil will also discourage flies in your kitchen; they dislike its strong odour.

Time and care taken to eliminate pests from your herbs will repay you with healthy foliage and roots, untainted by chemicals or poisons.

Soil Fertility

Farmers and gardeners all over the world know that to grow leafy green vegetables, annuals with sturdy constitutions, and shrubs and perennials to their peak, a soil rich in all the necessary plant food has to be provided. Herbs can play an enormously important role in building up soil fertility and, by way of thanks, a healthy soil grows even better herbs, too.

Organic gardening associations, and those gardeners in many countries who follow organic methods, believe that to avoid the soil starvation and depletion resulting from unbalanced artificial fertilizing, and the consequent reduced ability of crops to withstand insect ravages and disease, natural means only of enriching the soil and maintaining its fertility should be used. "Organic gardening" means returning to the earth everything taken from it in the form of decomposing animal and vegetable matter in a *natural form* which the plants can use. In Nature, fallen leaves, twigs, roots, grasses, and animal droppings, even the bones of dead animals and the microscopic bodies of the bacteria living in the soil, are returned to it, and slowly decompose to form the balanced plant nutrients necessary to keep forests and pastureland alive.

The so-called "complete fertilizers" of unnatural origin give (like some drugs) an initial boost; but much recent investigation has found that the soil, after this type of shot-in-the-arm, is left actually poorer than ever, and no increased applications of chemical fertilizers can restore vitality and life to it. Moreover, much of the mineral and chemical content of these fertilizers is in a form the plants can not easily assimilate. Composting and building up again with organic matter and humus can slowly, over a matter of many seasons, restore to the soil the fertility it has lost; but this is a long-term solution, and commercial growers can go broke while waiting for it to be effective.

The obvious answer is to prevent the soil's rape by artificial chemical additives, and to grow the produce organically in the first place, trying to duplicate Nature wherever possible. Food crops so grown are no danger to health, and contain many times more nutritional value.

Many publications are available to the keen gardener or commercial grower, setting out various methods of composting. One available free from the Department of Agriculture in New South Wales is *Building up Fertility in the Garden*; and although it does not follow the organic method closely its wealth of proven factual field experience by qualified aggronomists and agriculturalists gives much food for thought. *Fertility without Fertilizers*, a book issued by the Henry Doubleday Research Association, Bocking, Braintree, Essex, goes much farther into the making of the *organic* compost so necessary for natural growth. Here you will find much more thought-provoking research into the use of herbs and other natural agents for speeding up the process of composting.

Read as much as you can on organic gardening methods. It should be the far-sighted aim of farmers and gardeners not only to produce an immediate crop of better vegetables and fruit, or blooms the size of soup-plates for the annual horticultural show, but to build up in the soil the natural reserves of fertility that in a matter of a few seasons will not only make less work for them (a rich soil needs little or no attention), but will save them money normally spent on chemical fertilizers and sprays, as the crops' resistance to disease and insect attack is increased when grown under natural conditions. The humus and organic matter thus returned to the soil brings with it the "helpers", the earthworms, the micro-organisms and bacteria that keep the soil healthy and alive and break down the decomposing vegetable and animal matter into an easily assimilable form which the plants can then use.

In this book, it is not my intention to go step by step through the making of compost, but to tell you how herbs can be added to it as catalysts, contributing their concentrated minerals and other elements to make a compost that not only breaks down in half the time but is approximately twice as beneficial as one made without herbs.

Comfrey is the compost enricher *par excellence*. Its chemical composition is almost the same as that of farmyard manure, and its high natural calcium and nitrogen content and its quick decomposition make it a very necessary addition to each bin of compost. I build up my bins in layers as spent material becomes available, then turn the contents into a second bin, mixing comfrey leaves and stalks, well chopped, through the pile as I do so. Dolomite and a layer of sandy soil are spread through at intervals, and at the same time I add to the bin other herbs in varying quantities.

Yarrow is the catalyst. Work done in England and West Germany has proved that a "homeopathic dose" of 1 part in 10,000 of yarrow, added to each bin, is the most effective quantity. One or two tiny leaves, snipped finely and well-mixed through, are enough to "send off" about one or two cubic yards of compost material. Larger quantities of yarrow do not improve this process. On the contrary, they are not as speedy. So have faith, and add only this minute quantity.

Camomile is very rich in natural calcium, and essential for a "healthy" compost bin. It will stop excessive acidification, and keep the decomposing material sweet as well. Valerian, a little-known herb, is another asset to the soil. It stimulates phosphorus activity in the earth around it, and added to the compost is very valuable. Tansy, with its high proportion of potassium, ensures this necessary element is present, too, in large quantities. Nettles, the stinging little monsters often found around poultry farms, give their contribution of iron, and a catalytic action as well. Dandelion is another potent source of minerals, and can be added as often as you feel impelled to root it out of pathways or flowerbeds.

Add the green parts of all these herbs and the flowers as well if you have them. Roots are perhaps better left out, unless you are an experienced compost-maker; there will be less chance of incomplete breakdown. My own compost bins are ready about six weeks after the herbs are added and mixed well through, and a coarse sweet-smelling black organic "stew" is then ready to be spread over the soil and lightly dug in.

Animal manures can also be added to the composting material, but unless the urine as well as the faeces is present, the nitrogen content is much lower. Droppings from battery-kept, pellet-fed hens are not worth as much as deep litter from free-range birds, where straw or some similar material absorbs their urine as well. Animal manures are only as rich as the diet and general health of the animal concerned.

I like blood and bone as a companion for compost. Dug through the loosened soil when originally preparing it for perennial planting, it provides what would have been found in untampered-with Nature, a slowly releasable reservoir of bone, hair and decomposed "innards" and tissue, deep in the soil. It is rich in phosphorus, too, as well as having concentrated nitrogen and other trace elements.

Composting eliminates the so-called "waste" accumulated in the kitchen from vegetable and fruit peelings, eggshells, and remnants from herbal tea brews; it uses all soft garden waste, leaves from deciduous trees, spent annuals, and herb tops of all kinds. If you dry your own herbs, don't keep them on the shelf longer than a twelvemonth. Tip them through your compost, and put up another batch.

When you see the good results obtained by using organic compost, you will wonder why man has spent so much time and effort trying to improve on Nature's existing complete-ness. At one English garden showplace, Arkley Manor, an area of 7½ acres has for the past ten years been neither forked, spaded or dug, but organic compost has been spread over the surface of the soil at regular intervals. The results should con-vince even the most hardened champion of "Super" and constant back-breaking work with surface cultivation.

Natural dolomite, organic vegetable material, animal bone and hair, and the added powers of herbs, will give your garden or vegetable patch the life and vitality Nature intended.

THE HERBS

Angelica

Archangelica officinalis UMBELLIFERAE

Angelica is one of the oldest-known herbs. It is a native of cold countries, Russia and Lithuania and Iceland, and as far south as Germany. It is classified as a biennial, but if it is not allowed to flower and is cut back hard it will grow as a true perennial.

The legends about angelica are many. It was introduced into England in the sixteenth century with already a wide reputation on the Continent as a powerful remedy for coughs, colds and rheumatic complaints—all the troubles of the cold, damp climates in which it grows naturally and, as Nature has ordained, where it is most useful to man.

In Europe, it flowers on St Michael the Archangel's day, 8th May, and it figured in many rites and rituals for this festival. In England it gained a strong reputation as a stomach strengthener, and was used extensively, the roots in particular being chewed as a protection from the plague. Angelica root was said to actually cure even after infection had already taken place, and it was an ingredient in the "Four Thieves' Vinegar", a concoction of powerful herbs drunk by four robbers who pillaged the bodies of those dead from the plague, and maintained apparent immunity themselves.

In Norway, bread was often made using the dried powdered roots, but all parts of the plant are valuable, the leaves to use dried in pot-pourri (pick them before flowering commences), and the stems and bark stripped and candied, or cooked with rhubarb to take away its tart taste. The seeds are used to flavour liqueurs such as Chartreuse, and are also used commercially in perfumes.

For the gardener, growing angelica is easy once the initial problem is solved—that of the extremely short viability period of the seeds. Seeds should really be planted within several days of their being ripe on the parent plant, so if someone sells you or gives you angelica seed, try to determine when it was harvested. Seeds available from any reputable seedsman are usually treated and sealed at the source of supply to preserve their viability, but once the seal is broken they quickly lose germinating power. So try to track down a young plant, put it in your garden, and when the seeds are ripe distribute them among all your gardening friends. That way you should create an "angelica pool", with some seed always available. The plant will often self-sow if the seed is allowed to drop naturally, so you may have small plants to distribute as well.

Angelica is one herb that grows better in broken shade, and needs plenty of moisture to keep the young stems fast-growing and succulent. Plant the seeds 1 inch deep in the open garden or ½ inch deep in seed boxes in the autumn after gathering, and the young plants should be ready to set out in the spring. Nip out the centre to keep the plant bushy, or cut the main stem and let the side stems grow. Deeply dug soil is essential for this plant, for it can grow to 6 or 8 feet in suitably moist, well-fed soil.

Here is a recipe for candying the young stems, to produce those bits of sugary green to top that special-occasion cake.

Crystallized Angelica Stems.
Boil short (4-inch) lengths of fresh green stems, picked during the second year of growth, in water until just tender. Remove, and strip off outer skin, then return to the water and boil until green and not too soft. Drain and weigh the stems. Using 1 lb. of sugar to 1 lb. of fruit, cover with this sugar and let stand for 24 hours. Then boil the stems in the syrup until it is clear. Drain, dust with sugar, and dry on greaseproof paper in a cool oven. Cool, and store in glass screw-topped jars.

Rhubarb Pie
Here is a recipe for those who dislike the sharp taste of rhubarb, but appreciate all its iron.

Pastry for a 9-inch pie shell (wholemeal flour is delightful in this)
3½ to 4 cups sliced raw rhubarb
1 lemon (skin and pith removed) sliced
Several young stems of angelica sliced very thin
1¼ cups brown or raw sugar
2 tablespoons wholemeal flour mixed with the sugar

Line a pie-plate with the rolled-out pastry. Sprinkle one-third of the flour-sugar mixture over the crust. Arrange a layer of rhubarb and angelica, scatter lemon slices over, sprinkle with the flour-sugar mix. Repeat the layers until all ingredients are used. Cover with pastry lattice (it makes a juicy pie), and bake at 375 degrees for 50 to 60 minutes.

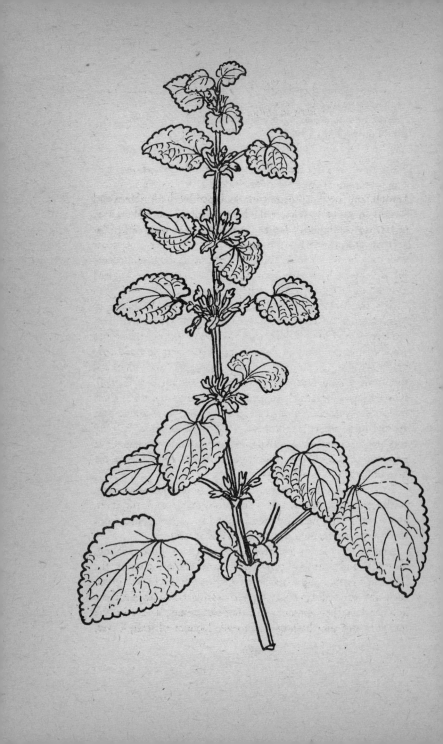

Lemon Balm

Melissa officinalis LABIATAE

Lemon, or "bee" balm, known and used by the Arabians and Greeks in ancient times, is a cheerful, sunny herb. Its name comes from the Greek for bee, *melissa*, and it was planted by apiarists around the hives to enable the bees to navigate their way back home. Its scent appears to be one of the most powerful and pleasant to any bee-"nose", and it was also rubbed around inside new hives to persuade the bees to stay.

Any plant bringing bees to a garden was very valuable in former times to the home gardener, as honey was the main sweetener used for foodstuffs, and its health-giving properties were well understood by the ancients. Gardeners and orchardists today who use cumulative and long-lasting toxic chemical sprays are killing not only predatory insects but bees as well. It is asking a bit much to expect bumper crops from their undoubtedly insect-free vegetables and fruit if there are no bees around to pollinate the flowers! One of the organic "safe by morning" sprays (see p. 36) applied at dusk after the bees have gone home will kill only the troublesome insects and leave the bees unharmed the next day.

So if you want heavy harvesting from your orchard or farm, plant lemon balm around the rows of vegetables and fruit trees, and bring all the bees for miles around to gather pollen from its flowers and fertilize your own crops as well.

Arabian physicians credited the herb with great healing, soothing and calming powers. It was known also as the "scholar's herb", and a tea brewed from the leaves was given each day to students studying for examinations, to clear the head and sharpen memory and understanding. To make the tea, pour one pint boiling water over 1 ounce of fresh leaves, infuse for five minutes, cool, strain, and drink several cups each day. Balm leaves can also be crushed and added to your cannister of China tea if you are still a confirmed addict.

The learned scholars of ancient times placed balm astrologically under the power of Jupiter, as a strong blood and heart restorative. The leaves of the herb, crushed, boiled, then mixed with oil, were used as a poultice for boils.

Balm is a member of the mint family, and can be propagated by root division in the autumn or spring, or from the tiny seed in the spring only. Soak the seed in warm water for 24 hours before planting, as the outside covering is hard and this will help it to germinate. You can also layer the stems as shown on p. 23. The seeds keep their germinating power for years.

The plant can grow some three feet high in a wide-spreading clump, and likes room around it to ensure full sunshine and freedom from a virus that can sometimes discolour the leaves. In cooler districts, lemon balm may die down altogether in the winter, but will come again in the spring. Cut the dead stems off several inches above the ground. The new growth will come from the base of these old stems.

Balm leaves dried keep their fragrance for a long period, and dry very successfully hung in bunches of stems about 12 inches long, about 5 or 6 stems to the bunch. Use only the older woody stems for drying, not the tender new growth.

Give it full sunshine, good soil and enough water, and an honoured place in your garden, and be rewarded by its many uses.

Try this cooling summer drink: To the juice of half a lemon add several balm leaves and several mint leaves crushed, then fill the glass with half apple juice and half lemonade.

Lemon Balm Stuffing

From Rennaissance times comes this old recipe for a piquant stuffing for duck.

Stuff the washed dried duck with the following mixture: an equal quantity of tart apples peeled and coarsely chopped, and uncooked stoned prunes. Chop well a good handful of lemon balm leaves, and mix all together. Stuff loosely inside the duck, and roast as required. This mixture absorbs and breaks down the fatty texture of the duck flesh, as well as being a delightful seasoning. Puncture the bird in all the fatty places, and allow the juices of the stuffing to penetrate.

Bananas with Strawberries
Try this variation on a hot banana dish which can be made in only a few minutes.

6 or 8 firm bananas
¼ cup brown sugar
8 or 10 lemon balm leaves, chopped finely
1 tablespoon rum or brandy
Fresh strawberries

Peel, and slice the bananas in half crossways. Heat a little butter in a heavy frying pan or oven-top cooking dish, and sauté the bananas lightly. Add the sugar, stirring well, then the rum and the lemon balm leaves. Quickly add the fresh strawberries, heat all through and serve at once. Delicious over vanilla ice-cream!

Lemon Balm Jelly
For a children's party (or a small dinner party), the colours of the following sweet make a gay splash to round off the meal.

½ oz. gelatine
¼ pint hot water
½ oz. raw sugar
¾ pint milk
Small handful chopped lemon balm leaves

Dissolve gelatine in the hot water, add the sugar and lemon balm leaves and stir till sugar is dissolved, then cool slightly and strain. When lukewarm, add the milk, and colour half the mixture pink if desired. Allow to set in shallow trays. Cut into cubes when set, and mix with cubes of mint jelly or green jelly.

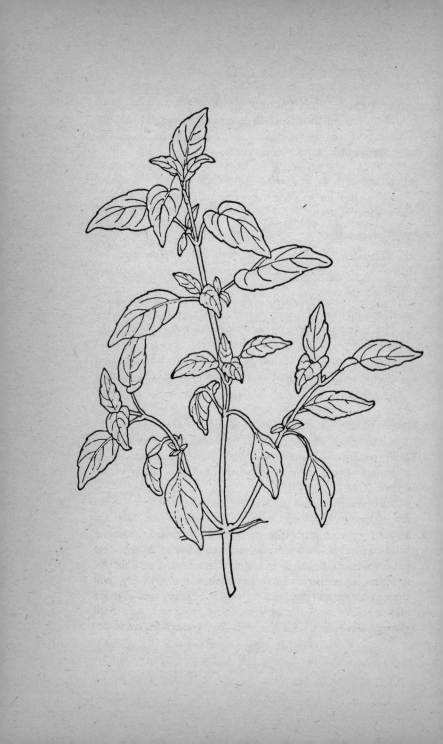

Basil

Sweet Basil *Ocymum basilicum*

Bush Basil *Ocymum minimum* LABIATAE

Basil has been called the king of all the herbs. Its name has been attributed to two different origins, some writers saying it comes from *basileus*, Greek for "king", but *basilicus*—basilisk, the old name for serpent—could refer to its reputation for counteracting poison from the bite or sting of a venomous creature.

The plant originally came from India, where it was sacred to Vishnu and Shiva, and a pot grew in every courtyard. By some, it was called the "herb of poverty", giving its protection to those poor and in want.

As its use spread into the Mediterranean countries, its legends grew and changed. In Italy, it stood for "love", and was called "Kiss me, Nicholas"; while in Greece it meant "hate", and a sprig given to a man meant "Be wary, someone is plotting against you." The Greeks and Romans very seldom agreed about anything. It also figured in Jewish lore, sprigs of basil being held in the hand to give strength when fasting. All its legendary users agreed that it was its *strength* that was so impressive.

Basil is easy to grow in frost-free places, needing only open sun and protection from wind for its brittle stems. Sow the round blue-black seeds in early to late spring, and the strong bright leaves should be through in 4 to 10 days. A light blue gelatinous film forms over the seed when it is touched by moisture before germinating, but the seeds, if kept dry, will keep their viability for many years. The young seedlings are easy to transplant, but keep a watch for snails and slugs. Basil grows quickly, and soon you will have enough leaves to use whenever required. Pinch out the centre stem as the plant grows, and let the side stems grow to keep it bushy. Water *in the heat of the day*: basil thrives only if its leaves as well as its roots have moisture.

Strictly speaking, both varieties are annuals; but if you live in a warm, frost-free area, you may be able to cut the bushes back hard in late autumn and have them come again the next spring. Try growing basil in a courtyard, it loves the reflected heat from stone or brick: and its perfume will be at its best. In India, it is grown as a true perennial; the frost-free, warm climate of the plains and the abundant water keep it in ideal condition. However, it is so easy to raise from seed and so quick to grow that it is advisable usually to sow fresh seed or buy new plants each spring.

Sweet Basil has large (2 to 2½-inch) leaves, and is most suitable for outdoors. Bush Basil will also grow just as well outside, but its small (½ inch) leaves and more compact growth make it an ideal herb to grow in a pot. The Sweet Basil has a slightly stronger flavour, but both are delicious.

If you require basil to use as far into the winter as possible, sow some seed in mid-summer, transplant the seedlings into their own pots (medium size will do), and when the autumn chill starts to creep into the night air install a pot in a sunny corner indoors. Water its foliage as well as the soil, or you may come home from a day out, the house closed and warm, to find your basil has "fainted". Once you see a plant in this condition, you will know just how apt is the description. But never fear, moisture will revive it.

The succulent soft leaves of basil do not dry well for the home gardener, needing the more sophisticated apparatus of commercial drying ovens. But, if you wish, preserve your basil in the fullness of its summer flavour by cutting just before the dainty white flowers begin to bud, and store it in the traditional Indian way as follows: Put a layer of stems and leaves covering the bottom of an earthenware crock, or casserole (with a lid). Then sprinkle a layer of salt to cover the leaves. Repeat this until you have used up all your basil, making salt the last layer, and put the lid on the crock. When you want to use the basil, just shake the salt off the sprig, wash and use as required. You can also cover the fresh-cut stems with pure olive oil to preserve them. Oil is often an ingredient in recipes using basil, so the taste will not be out of place.

Basil grown in a pot indoors will help to discourage flies. It is one of the few herbs that gives off its perfume without the leaves being bruised. Even the dry dead stems of the plant, quite brown and finished, will still have the same powerful scent.

The medicinal uses of basil are many. From very ancient times it has been used to clear the head and brain, and it was an ingredient in snuff. The oil was often used in perfumes and rubbed on the temples to dispel headaches, as thyme oil was. There is an old supersitition that women will not eat from a dish that has had a sprig of basil placed underneath it. Perhaps an aid to dieting?

Recipes using basil are legion. It can flavour almost any Mediterranean or Asian dish to advantage, particularly when ingredients from the warm sunny areas are used. It should always be used fresh, or added at the last minute if cooking, for the flavour becomes very bitter if it is heated for long periods. Basil is, by legend, a "herb of Mars", a very powerful "masculine" one. Use it sparingly. One or two leaves of the sweet variety will flavour a whole dish. Try steeping a *small* handful of the herb in hock or chablis at room temperature for 24 hours, then chill again before serving. Try it in a salad bowl, one or two leaves chopped over fresh tomatoes, or egg dishes.

Omelette Sauce
Here is a Basque recipe.

4 small tomatoes
1½ tablespoons olive oil
Raw sugar
Basil
Lemon juice (1 teaspoon), salt

Chop the tomatoes, simmer in the olive oil, sprinkle lightly with the sugar, add salt. Simmer 5 minutes. Add chopped basil, simmer one minute, add the lemon juice, and blend all together well. Pour over omelette.

Pesto Sauce
From Genoa comes the traditional sauce for all pasta dishes.

4 tablespoons fresh chopped basil
2 tablespoons ground pine nuts (or walnuts)
3 garlic cloves, crushed
3 tablespoons Parmesan cheese
5 tablespoons olive oil
2 tablespoons melted butter

Pound basil, nuts and garlic in a mortar with the pestle (hence the name). When quite crushed, add the cheese and pound till a thick purée is formed. Slowly add oil and butter bit by bit, grinding as you go. Blend all well together. The sauce can be gently heated for a few moments before pouring over the pasta.

Greek Mézé
Here is another delicacy from the Mediterranean, an appetizer, served on hot toasted bread fingers.

2 oz. black olives (stoned) finely minced
1 hardboiled egg (discard most of the white)
2 tablespoons olive oil
1½ teaspoons lemon juice.
Several leaves chopped basil
1 tablespoon fried onion

Blend all well together, and refrigerate till needed. Can be made the day before, but if so add the basil an hour before serving, and bring to room temperature.

A Sauce with Basil for Spaghetti
2 or 3 zucchini
1 green pepper
1 crushed garlic clove

4 tablespoons olive oil
2 large tomatoes
salt and freshly ground pepper
1 tablespoon anchovy paste
a few capers
several black olives
4 to 6 leaves sweet basil
8 oz. spaghetti

Sauté the zucchini, green pepper and garlic lightly in the oil. Then add tomatoes, salt and pepper, and cook slowly for about 10 minutes over low heat. Add the anchovy paste, capers, olives and basil and cook a further 5 minutes. Pour this mixture over the cooked and drained spaghetti, and serve piping hot.

Bergamot

Monarda didyma LABIATAE

Sweet Bergamot, Horsemint, or Oswego Tea—all refer to a shade-loving perennial herb, a native of the New World first reported by Dr Nicholas Monardez, a Spanish physician, in his book *Joyfull newes out of the newe founde world* published in England in 1577. (Incidentally in this book he also first described and illustrated the tobacco plant, so perhaps his services to mankind are somewhat doubtful.)

Bergamot leaves and flowers were used freely as a tea substitute in North America and, since the herb was first found near Lake Oswego, this is where it gained one of its names. It is a member of the mint family, and has a period of total dormancy from late autumn till early spring. Put a stake near the roots to remind you where your plant is, so winter digging will not remove it altogether.

In spring, up will come the first tiny fragrant leaves, then long upright stems that will grow to about two feet in height, of similar habit to mint, with the soft velvety leaves set opposite on the stalk. In midsummer, the brilliant red flowering heads appear, a cluster of tiny trumpet-shaped blossoms reminiscent of a small-scale honeysuckle. The bees love the plant, but so do the caterpillars and snails; so keep it sprayed at the first sign of a nibbled leaf and you will have a flamboyant addition to your salad bowl: several of the scarlet flower heads as a garnish, and a few chopped leaves in the salad itself.

When picking the leaves for a hot "brew" (the usual quantity, a small handful to a large cup of water) make sure you don't finish up with caterpillar tea! Green caterpillars have a perfect camouflage on this plant, and constant vigilance is necessary; but the distinctive appearance and flavour are worth all the time you spend on it. Give it soil rich in leaf-mould and plenty of water. In its natural state it grows in the damp, rich woodland soils where falling leaves each autumn make a perfect winter blanket for it, and their decomposition by the spring gives it necessary food. It will grow happily in the partial shade of taller plants as long as there is room for its roots to forage in damp soil. The rather brittle stems may need light tying and staking to keep the plant neat, for the flowers are rather heavy and tend to pull the branch down. Don't let that crimson showpiece trail in the dirt.

Like all the mints, bergamot contains thymol, a natural antiseptic, and the tea is very soothing for sore throats. Dried leaves and flower heads can also be put in the canister with ordinary tea to give it a flavour boost.

Pork Chops in Cider Sauce
Bergamot has a natural affinity for pork dishes, and this recipe is a traditional early North American one.

4 thick pork chops, fat removed
2 teaspoons chopped bergamot
Oil, salt, pepper
¼ pint cider
Chopped gherkins, capers

Use a small sharp knife and score small slits in the chops on each side. Mix enough oil with the salt and pepper and chopped bergamot to make a paste, and rub into the slits in the meat. Leave for one hour. Then put chops under grill, and cook about 10 minutes each side under moderate heat, saving all the juices from the grill pan. Remove to shallow oven-proof dish. Pour the cider and juices over the chops, sprinkle top with chopped gherkins and capers, and brown for 5 minutes in a moderately hot oven. Serve with grilled pineapple or apple rings.
Bergamot can be propagated by root division after the first year, the clump divided in early spring as soon as the first leaves show. In any case, it should be dug up every three or four years, thinned out and replanted.

60

An orange salad can be given a piquant lift using freshly picked bergamot leaves. Peel and remove all the pith from the oranges, cut in neat wedges and pile in a small bowl, placing lightly bruised bergamot leaves in among the orange segments. Leave for an hour, then serve on a bed of lettuce with chopped bergamot leaves sprinkled over the top. The salad can be lightly dressed with apricot-kernel oil, or any bland salad oil, if you wish.

Borage

Borago officinalis BORAGINACEAE

The "Herb of Gladness", borage was a favourite of the ancient writers and scholars. The leaves, and sometimes the flowers, too, were steeped in wine and drunk as a general tonic, and an uplift for mind and spirit. It is believed to be the Nepenthe of Homer, used to dispel sorrow when mixed with wine, and it has perhaps a similar use today in Pimm's No. 1 Cup, which it flavours.

Pliny christened it "Euphrosium", and wrote that it made men merry and glad. It also gained the reputation of giving courage as well as joy, and became a flower symbol for courage. The brilliant blue starry blooms were embroidered on scarves by the womenfolk and these were presented to warriors before battle. In the age of chivalry in England, a cup of borage tea was often drunk by competitors before tournaments and jousts.

Borage is an easy annual to grow, and can be sown right through the year in warm frost-free areas; but if you live in a district that gets frosts it is best to sow in spring, with another planting in early summer. When scorched by frosts, the plant degenerates to black, brittle untidiness, and this may have been its state when Gerard described it as having "leaves of a black or swarte green colour".

The biggish, bomb-shaped seeds should be sown covered by $\frac{1}{4}$ inch of soil in the garden or $\frac{1}{8}$ inch in seed boxes. They sprout readily, with almost 100 per cent germination, and should be through the soil in 3 to 8 days. The seeds will also self-sow very readily, so if you start with one plant, although it is an annual, you will soon have many small seedlings about your garden. Put borage in full sunshine, keep it well-watered

63

in the early stages, but do not feed it too heavily or you will get huge clumps with many leaves but no flowers. Underfeeding, if anything, is better. The hairy greyish-green leaves can sting with their sharp little needles when you pick them, so handle with gloves and care. Washing under cold water for several minutes before use makes them more tractable. Borage leaves are not recommended for drying at all for the home gardener.

Try several leaves, chopped, to make tea in the usual manner. Pour a cup of boiling water over, and let stand for 5 minutes, or simmer the leaves in water for 3 or 4 minutes (do not boil), strain, and drink steaming hot with a few drops of lemon juice added. The herb has a great deal of saline mucilage, and its salty taste can be a valuable additive to mineral-salt-free diets. Indeed, it is one of the main ingredients, with kelp, in many vegetable salts. The same natural saline content helps reduce temperatures and fevers when the drink is taken hot, and promotes kidney health and activity when used fresh in salads. Chop the cucumber-flavoured leaves finely after washing well: your family or guests may not enjoy a large lump of hairy borage as much as tiny, more palatable pieces. It is very rich in potassium, needed for healthy tissues, bowels, kidneys and liver, and has large quantities of easily assimilable calcium as well. No wonder it kept those ancient warriors on their toes.

Borage was always classed as a herb of jolly Jupiter, a general blood and body strengthener. Its leaves, placed in a bowl of fruit punch, or liquid of any kind, will not only give that cool cucumber flavour, but will actually reduce its temperature.

Plant your borage in the rockery or somewhere a bit raised up from ground level. The starry blue flowers hang down in clusters, and you will be able to see them to advantage without getting down on all fours. The flowers can be candied, too, for an unusual garnish on cakes, fruit salads or sweets. Pop a couple, together with fresh mint leaves, on top of a plain egg custard served in individual crystal dishes, and watch your hostess reputation rise overnight. Here are two different methods of crystallizing the flowers:

1. Pick the flowers when barely open, lay on waxed paper, brush all over each blossom with beaten egg white using a small soft paintbrush, then dust castor sugar over through a fine sieve, and let dry. When quite dry and hard, store in airtight jars, lined with grease-proof paper.

2. Pick flowers when barely open. Wash them and spread out to dry. Make a syrup of 1 cup sugar and ¾ cup water, and boil until it spins a thread (25 degrees on a candy thermometer). Pour into a heat-resistant bowl (not glass), and place in a bed of crushed ice to cool it quickly. When syrup begins to crystallize, dip blossoms in one at a time, holding them with fine tweezers by the base, and thoroughly coat with the syrup. Shake off the surplus, put on greaseproof paper, and dry. As they begin to harden, dust with castor sugar through a fine sieve. Store in airtight jars when thoroughly dry.

Borage has been planted by commercial strawberry growers to assist in the growth of the young plants. The borage is also helped by the strawberry plants, and grows extremely well. Thus the two are true companion plants, each stimulating the growth of the other. A plant of borage every 12 to 18 feet along the rows has been found a suitable distance. There is room for much experimentation and tabulation of such companion plants that can be of value to commercial growers. Several instances are mentioned in this book, and if you have any such experiences with your own gardening the Bio-Dynamic Farming and Gardening Association Inc., of Stroudsberg, P.A., U.S.A., will be very glad to hear of them. Only by collecting information from farmers and gardeners all over the world can such results be evaluated, and as world food problems increase any methods of increasing crop growth and yield can be of great importance. Who knows, your own "helpful hint", based on proved experience, could help cancel out in the long run some of the problems of feeding the earth's population.

Millet Pilaff
If your teeth are your own, and you enjoy using them, try this recipe, a reputed favourite of the ancient Persian kings; but

make sure you buy the millet seed for human consumption, not millet *birdseed*, or the husks will be very unpalatable—more like lead shot than a culinary delicacy. The French White Millet is the best variety, and your health food store should have it.

1 cup millet
1 tablespoon olive oil
¾ cup cold water
Salt and pepper
1 tablespoon soy sauce
1 crushed garlic clove
2 fine chopped borage leaves
Spring onions, chopped
Thin slices raw button mushrooms
Young uncooked green peas

Wash millet, and drain. Heat the oil in a large heavy pan and fry the millet until golden over medium heat, tossing over occasionally. Pour in the cold water, salt, soy sauce, and garlic. Cook gently till water is absorbed, grains separate and dry. Remove garlic. Add remainder of ingredients, stir through to heat quickly, and serve at once.

Antipasto

Try this Italian hors-d'oeuvre as an appetizer, or do as the Romans do and have a different breakfast for a change. Serve with crisp bread sticks. Very low on calories!

12 button mushrooms, sliced lengthwise
1 oz. uncooked green beans
2 stalks celery, cut in strips 2 inches long, ½ inch wide
½ green capsicum, slivered
½ oz. walnut halves
Cauliflower florets, sliced ¼ inch thick
1 small carrot, slivered

Marinade
¾ cup wine vinegar
1 clove garlic, crushed
Pinch oregano, bunch parsley
3 borage leaves, chopped
1 tablespoon raw sugar

Bring marinade to the boil, cool, shake with 5 tablespoons olive oil in a glass jar until well blended (or use blender). Pour over vegetables in a covered earthenware crock, and stir several times in the following two days. Drain, and serve on platter. It is advisable to provide small forks with this dish, as the vegetables may be a little too oily to handle. For a variation, add some fennel or dill seeds to the mixture instead of the oregano.

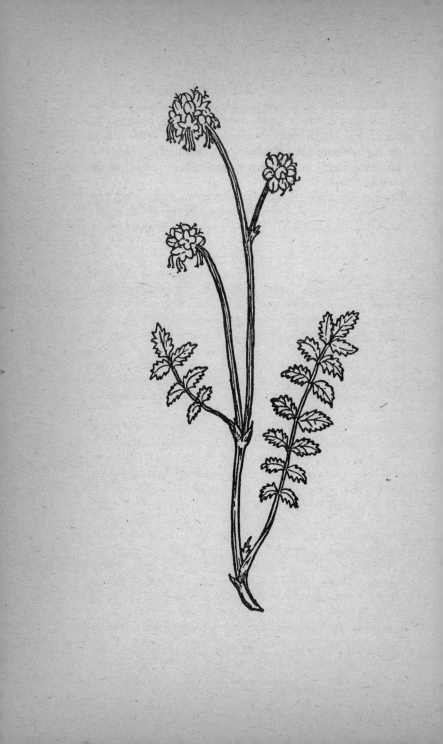

Salad Burnet

Sanguisorba minor ROSACEAE

This plant I call the "fountain herb", because it grows just like the fountains on those old bird-baths; the outside leaves lie down towards the ground and the new leaves spring upright in the middle. It is a perennial, and stays green and fresh all winter, a boon to the herb gardener.

If you are a vegetarian and like your salads all the year round, plant salad burnet. Its cool cucumber flavour and delicate green leaves add a fillip to those winter greens when other salad vegetables and fruit are not so plentiful. You will be doing your health a favour, too, for burnet, like borage, is a general blood purifier and tonic, with a cooling relaxing effect. It helps to reduce the indigestibility of cucumber, and is often used with or instead of this vegetable for people with digestive troubles. The chopped leaves can be added to herb vinegars too (see p. 25-6).

The plant grows easily from seed, and will self-sow if in the right conditions. It is quite a small, compact herb, some 12 to 15 inches high, in a tidy little rosette, and would be very suitable for a window box or small pot, and ideal for home-unit dwellers who want to grow a few herbs in a limited space. Pull off the old leaves from underneath if you wish to keep it tidy for pot cultivation; but if it is in the open garden the old leaves will just decompose happily out of sight under the fountain of new leaves.

The flowers are not impressive: long slender stems with a tight knot of tiny green florets at the tip. Keep these nipped off unless you want seed to start off new plants; the flavour of the leaves is better if the plant is not allowed to flower.

Ways of using salad burnet are more varied than the often

69

rather limited culinary uses of the stronger, more aromatic herbs. It has no perfume at all, so it can be added to any salad or vegetable dish without clashing with other strong flavours. It is seldom used with meat, and never cooked. Try it chopped over asparagus or steamed celery, or as a garnish with a cheese and pineapple salad. Add it to potato salad with parsley and chives, or place a small leaf sprig on sliced cucumber or tomato. Its bland flavour will not offend anyone.

In a fruit cup or claret cup, burnet leaves look fresh and inviting. Add them to fruit salad, too; and they are very compatible with fresh strawberries.

So use your own favourite recipes, and freshen them up with salad burnet. Remember always to use it fresh. It can be quite bitter and unpleasant if cooked.

The herb is very hardy, and will recover from a drought or a flood with equanimity. If you wish to increase your stock of plants, set out several salad burnet near each other and allow some to flower while keeping others to pick for culinary use. The seeds will eventually drop and re-sow themselves, and small plants will spring up around the old ones. This process does not seem to work so well if only a single plant sets seed. Salad burnet is gregarious, and flourishes best in a small colony.

Green-Leaf Sauce
Pick some fresh soft greens from your herb garden or vegetable patch (salad burnet, sorrel, celery leaves, chives, parsley, silver beet, spinach, broccoli, etc.), chop them finely and add to a plain, rather thick white sauce. Stir and heat through, then serve over wholemeal toast or with brown rice

Cucumber Sandwiches
Cut brown wholemeal bread in wafer-thin slices, and butter lightly. Wash the cucumber well, and score the skin lengthwise with a fork. Rub the cut half of a lemon briskly over it, slice it thinly crosswise, and fill the sandwiches, sprinkling the cucumber slices with finely chopped salad burnet and a few chopped chives.

In the height of summer, when heavy, hot food is uninviting, a soup made from fruit and herbs can be a tempting appetizer to start your meal. Many different fruits can be used, but tart summer apples will always be a favourite.

Apple and Herb Soup

1 lb. cooking apples
Celery tops, finely chopped
½ cup raw sugar
Cinnamon, cloves
1 pint water
Shredded rind and juice of 1 lemon
Salad burnet leaves

Cook together the apples, celery, sugar and spices in the water, having first peeled and cored the apples and cut them into small dice to shorten the cooking time. Add the lemon rind and juice in the last few minutes of cooking, stirring well through the apple mixture, which should be cooked to a coarse mush. Set this aside to cool, and before serving add individual leaves of salad burnet and stir well through the soup. A few extra leaves can be used on top to garnish. If you wish to make this your whole meal, serve it with rye bread topped with a bland cottage cheese.

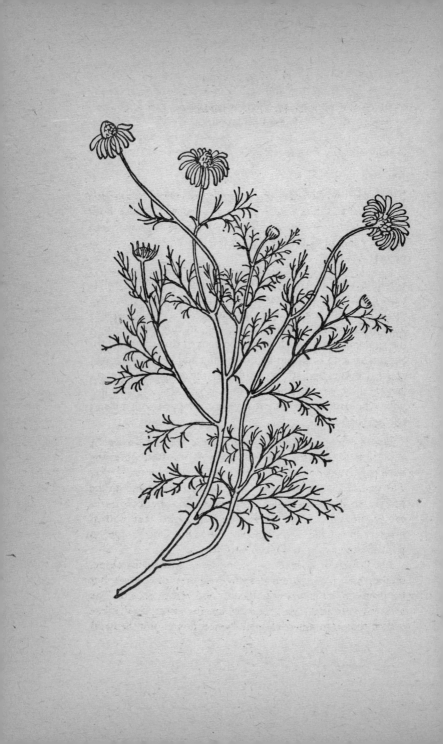

Camomile

Anthemis nobilis COMPOSITAE

There are two varieties of camomile, an annual (*Matricaria chamomilla*) and the creeping perennial (*Anthemis nobilis*). Both are used widely for camomile tea and for the lightening and conditioning of fair hair. The plants are extremely rich in natural calcium.

Perennial camomile is a ground cover, a feathery ferny-leaved little plant that flowers in its second year of growth. It has no particular likes or dislikes, but is best if not subjected to extremes of heat, cold or moisture. Average garden conditions suit it well and, having a prostrate habit of growth, it can be planted as a fragrant herb lawn, staying green all year round. One such lawn is still flourishing in Buckingham Palace grounds. The perfume hovers somewhere between apple and clove, and the lightest touch will release it. It is often called the "herb of humility", because it grows best when walked on, and indeed relishes this treatment.

Before planting a camomile lawn, weed the area *thoroughly*, if possible putting the top few inches of soil through a fine sieve to get out any previous grass roots or weed roots or bulbs. The stems of camomile grow close together above and on the ground, so weeds can be difficult to eradicate. Camomile lawns can be mowed. Set the blades somewhat higher than normal in order to cut the leaves but miss the stems. Don't forget to put the clippings onto the compost heap.

The flowers are a lovely yellow-centred white daisy shape, on short stems, and bloom all spring and most of summer, but the plants do not flower until their second year of growth. The yellow centre is the part from which the essential oil is extracted; but in commercial use the whole flower (not the stem)

73

is dried with as little bruising as possible. The flowers should be picked off from the stems by hand carefully or with tweezers, on a dry day. They dry even better if the previous two or three days have been dry, too. Picking in wet or very humid weather will result in brownish, discoloured flowers of very little use at all.

The herb can be raised from seed sown in the spring, but will take a little longer this way than by the usual root-division method. It is quite easy to lift a small clump and separate it into rooted pieces for setting out in a lawn or an edging patch in the garden. Plant these runners about 12 inches apart and, with the first growing season over, your lawn should be almost covered. You can top-dress lightly in summer if soil has been washed away by rain or watering and the stems are too far above the ground. This light top-dressing each season will help thicken up the growth.

Anthemis nobilis is English or Roman camomile. It was one of the nine sacred Saxon herbs, and was said to be under the sign of the Sun, a tribute to its very beneficial qualities. German camomile, too, was used for gastro-intestinal disorders as a soothing, warming, healing agent, and an aid to good digestion and sound sleep. It is often used as a children's tea, being very mild in its action. Some Continental hotels still serve it to their guests as a nightcap at suppertime. It has a distinctive flavour of its own, and a slightly "slippery" taste. It gives me the same sensation on my tongue as a fine silk does on my skin. Perhaps "slithery" would be a better description.

Two teaspoons of the dried flowers in a cup of water brewed in the usual way and taken at bedtime should ensure a happy digestive system and a good night's sleep.

The name of the herb comes from the Greek *chamai*—on the ground, and *melon*—an apple. The Spanish sherry Manzanilla is flavoured with camomile.

The pure oil of camomile, which is used in hair and skin preparations, is a beautiful blue when distilled, becoming greenish-brown on keeping. Here is a rinse for your hair which should improve both its colour and general health.

Fair Hair Rinse

Boil ½ ounce of dried camomile flowers in 1 pint of water for 20 minutes. Allow to cool, and use as a final rinse after all shampoo has been rinsed off thoroughly. Leave this rinse on the hair for a beautiful perfume, too. Natural blonde hair will be kept highlighted and beautiful.

Camomile Shampoo

Put 1 tablespoon of mild soapflakes (such as Lux), 1 tablespoon of borax, and 1 ounce of powdered camomile flowers into a basin. Add about ½ pint of hot water, and beat the ingredients until they form a thick lather. Wet the hair with warm water, and shampoo with this lather, massaging well into the scalp. Rinse once, and repeat. Rinse finally with warm water.

Camomile planted amongst other shrubs and annuals helps to keep them, and the soil near them, healthy and disease-free. It has often been called a plant "tonic". Use it around the edges and in the odd spaces in your herb garden. Camomile tea has also been found very useful for the gardener. In England recent testing has proved the findings of many home gardeners, that it will prevent "damping off" of seedlings. It is prepared for garden use by steeping a handful of dried blooms in cold water for several hours, then watering the solution over the seed boxes. Unfortunately there was no specification in the publication I read as to how much water to use with the handful of blooms, so this will be a matter of experiment for you. It will certainly not harm any plants at any reasonable concentration. I have found one pint of water the best amount to use myself, and no damping off of seedlings has resulted since its use.

Any tea left over can be poured over the compost heap. Camomile extends its tonic properties even here, and will help keep the bin sweet whilst adding its personal store of mineral content, especially calcium.

You can also make a brew of the tea and add it to your bath water, for any redness or inflammation of the skin. It is gentle and soothing for sunburn.

Catmint

Nepeta cataria LABIATAE

Catmint, or catnip, is a delicately perfumed shrubby perennial, growing some 2 to 3 feet high and about 3 feet across. It has pale soft-green serrated leaves set opposite on rather woody stems, and beautiful tiny creamy flowers with a mauve patch, growing in clusters at the stem tips for most of the spring and summer. If the bush is cut back hard after each flowering flush, it will come again with renewed vigour. The seed is tiny, and the best method for harvesting is to cut the ripe branch, shake it upside down in a plastic bag, and recover the seed by putting the resulting mixture of pods, stems and trash (and probably one or two bugs) through a fine tea strainer.

The plant can be propagated by dividing the clump, or severing some of the new outside growth from the side of the clump with a sharp spade and planting anew. Layering (see p. 23) is also a useful and time-saving way of increasing your plants.

In the eighteenth century tainted meat seemed to be the usual fare for those too poor to obtain regular fresh supplies. With no refrigeration, meat was salted or stored in cool rooms, in wired pantries or primitive "cooling boxes", and various methods were used to take away its strong rather off-putting taste and aroma. Catnip, being a native of Britain, was one source of a readily available, pleasant purifier for meat that was to be stewed. It was often cooked with the meat or steeped with it in water for many hours before cooking. Another way of purifying meat was quoted by Audet in 1818 in the *City and Country Cookbook*: "The best way to rescue meat with a bad taste: drop the meat into boiling water. When foam appears on the surface, remove from fire and drop in two red-hot coals.

When the coals have ceased to hiss, the meat is ready for use." Perhaps catmint was a more pleasant alternative.

Nowadays, catnip is not a culinary herb, but is valuable medicinally. A tea made in the usual way (see p. 64) from the leaves has been found very effective as a mild sedative, especially for children. Catmint tea is often mentioned in herbal therapy as being prescribed for the over-active child, or one who tosses and turns in bed or is subject to sleepwalking or nightmares. The tea taken hot brings out perspiration, and cold can be taken in a fruit drink. Like all natural medicine, the effect is not quick and spectacular but slower and more lasting. Regular use seems to be indicated to achieve results. The juice of the leaves has been given mixed with wine or treacle or honey to help inward bruising after any heavy fall. Put the leaves through the juicer for this if you wish to try it.

Catnip has long been used as a natural tonic and stimulant for cats, who often love to roll and revel in its foliage; but more particularly they love the root of the plant. If you own a cat, watch its behaviour when you dig around the roots or lift the clump for transplanting or dividing. It will go into ecstasies of delight. Chewing the root of catnip was said to make timid persons fierce and aggressive! Bees are attracted to the sweet-scented blossoms, so here's another herb to bring those pollen-laden friends to a market gardener's crops.

Sow the tiny seed of catnip in the autumn, give the plant room to grow, with sunlight and light soil, and keep a watchful eye out for caterpillars or grasshoppers.

There is also a garden variety of catmint (*Nepeta mussini*) with quite a different form of growth. It is a small rockery or edging plant, with grey-green foliage and lavender-coloured spikes of flowers. It grows in a dense little clump and can be very decorative in a pathway or warm sunny corner near a wall.

This plant has some of the medicinal value, but not all, of the other variety, and *Nepeta cataria* is the more valuable. Try planting this garden variety over your spring bulbs, then when the daffodils and hyacinths are flowering they will have a soft supporting carpet of green and mauve. When they die down, the catmint will still be there instead of just a bare space.

Nepeta mussini must also be cut back after flowering. The plant will grow somewhat straggly and wilted, and then the new growth will commence again from the centre. As soon as this is under way, cut off all the last season's old spent stems. You will probably find quite a few snails and slugs are thus deprived of a favourite haunt.

Try a vase of *Nepeta cataria* when it is in flower on your dining-room table. The delicate perfume will fill the room.

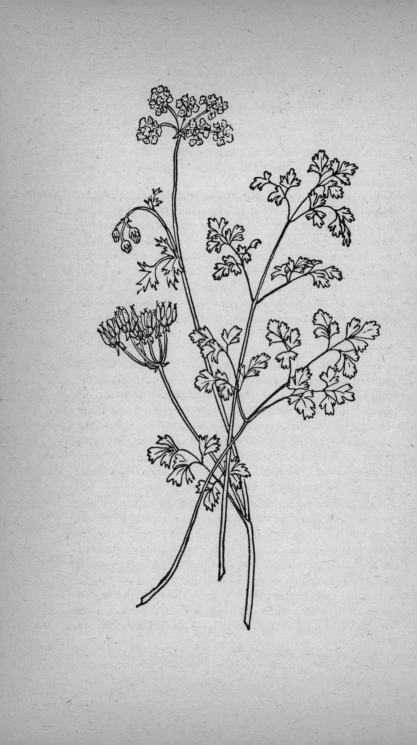

Chervil

Anthriscus cerefolium UMBELLIFERAE

Chervil might be called a flavour catalyst amongst other herbs. It has the unique property of adding to the flavour of any other herb in a dish while keeping its own slightly aromatic parsley-like taste, and should always be added to a *bouquet garni*. It has no perfume and, being delicate and small, is one herb that grows better inside than out. In appearance it is very like parsley, with light-green, soft, feathery leaves and tiny white flowers, which should be nipped off unless you require the plant to set seed for propagation. The leaves are ready for use about 6 to 8 weeks after sowing, and the more the young leaves are used the more bushy it will grow.

Growing chervil outdoors is a delicate operation: it needs dappled shade in summer and full sun (but no frost) in the colder months. The best place outside would be under the summer shade of a deciduous tree, and sheltered from winds. Then when autumn comes and the leaves of the tree fall the plants can take full advantage of the warm sun. My own chervil grows in a pot under the shelter and shade of wisteria. In the cooler months, protected from harsh winds by a fence, it gets all the sunshine it needs.

Chervil is an annual, and the life of individual plants is short; so sow seeds at regular intervals to ensure a good supply. It does not transplant very well, so it is one exception to my preference for sowing herbs in seed boxes first. Sprinkle some seeds on the surface of the soil in the pot or container in which it is to grow, and cover lightly with about ⅛ inch of potting mixture. Leave several plants to grow for seed, and several more for the table, cutting the leaves with small scissors when required. Never try to pick chervil leaves by hand, or you may

81

pull out the whole plant. Frail and delicate are the words for this herb.

The plants grown for seed will flower and the leaves go a lovely shade of pinkish-mauve when the seeds are ripe. Harvest the seed then, and re-sow as soon as possible. Chervil seed has limited keeping qualities, and is best when sown again quickly after ripening. So, using this system, you will have a self-perpetuating chervil factory.

If you wish to grow chervil indoors, it will do very well indeed. Hunt around the nurseries and garden stores, and find a decorative trough or large container (with drainage holes, of course, and preferably a saucer underneath). Follow the usual procedure of putting a layer of coarse gravel, crocks or other drainage material over the bottom inch of the container, then fill with a rich potting mixture, not tamping it down too hard, to within one inch of the top. Then sow the seeds as I have suggested. When the plants are in full growth transfer the trough or pot to your dining-table as a centrepiece, and let your guests snip off their own fresh leaves to add to a salad or to egg dishes.

Incidentally, chervil always germinates best if sown two or three days before the full moon.

The leaves, when cut, should always be used immediately, and can be added to almost any savoury dish at the last minute. The herb seems to have a natural affinity for eggs, and is traditionally used with omelettes and other egg dishes.

Asparagus-Chervil Filling
Here is a chervil-assisted filling for omelettes or pancakes.

Drain canned or fresh-cooked asparagus and heat quickly in a little butter. Add a handful of chopped chervil, heat through, and turn onto the omelette. Drizzle a little lemon juice over, drool, and eat.

Chervil has slight antibiotic properties. Eat as much of it as you fancy.

Quiche Lorraine can have chervil added for an unusual note in this otherwise traditional dish.

Quiche Lorraine

1 6-oz. packet flaky pastry
¼ pint milk
¼ pint cream
2 eggs
3 rashers bacon
chervil (3 scant tablespoons when chopped)

Line a deep flan or soufflé pan with the rolled-out pastry, then place this in the fridge until your filling is made. Beat the eggs, sauté the chopped bacon lightly, add the other ingredients and season to taste. Pour into the prepared pastry case and bake in a moderate to hot oven until the pastry is brown and the filling firm.

Chicory

Cichorium intybus COMPOSITAE

Strictly speaking, chicory is a pot-herb, almost a vegetable, but I have included it here because of its wonderful store of vitamins and minerals, and that liver- and gall-regulating substance, choline. It is very rich in calcium, copper and iron. It is such an easy trouble-free plant to grow, decorative if grown for its flowers in the herbaceous beds, useful as a winter vegetable if cooked, and a source of many essential body needs when eaten raw in a salad.

The variety known as Belgian or Brussels Chicory is the herb used very extensively in Europe. It is even grown as a rich fodder-crop for cattle in some parts of France and northern Italy. It grows rapidly, is a perennial, and is a very nutritive diet addition for man or beast.

Some people have probably heard of chicory only in "coffee and chicory"; and you may think, as I once did, that it is a cheap adulterant to add to coffee essence to bring down its price. Nothing could be farther from the truth. The canny French learnt from the Italians and Greeks, who learnt from the Asiatics: that heavy coffee drinking can have a very bad effect on the liver. So what more simple to those wise early "nutritionists" than to add a substance that helped the liver and gall action of the body—chicory. The roots are the parts used for the beverage, being roasted and ground at the end of the growing season, and either added to coffee or used instead of it, to make a very palatable drink.

The plant grows from 3 to 5 feet high if wanted for its flowers. The bright blue cornflower or daisy-shaped blooms open up along the tall flowering spikes each day. The time varies with different localities, but my flowers open at sunrise and close at 2 p.m. every day. Chicory was one of the plants included in the floral clock planted by Linnaeus, that great botanist and zoologist, on which the hours were marked by different plants' opening and closing times. It has been noted that the leaves of chicory always align themselves towards the north, and those interested in theosophy and metaphysics attribute great life-giving forces to the plant. Do not confuse this chicory with the vegetable, endive, which is often mistakenly called "chicory".

The seeds of chicory germinate easily, and keep their freshness for several years. The leaves are toothed, somewhat like the dandelion, which it resembles. If you are growing the plants as a vegetable, it is advisable to dig out a trench about 6 to 8 inches deep, and dig food and humus into the bottom layer of the trench; then set out the plants some 12 inches apart. As the leaves grow, and when about 6 to 12 leaves are showing, hill up the soil around each plant to about 5 or 6 inches, thus bringing the surface up to ground level once again. The plants need to be bleached in this way to remove the slightly bitter taste of the dark leaves. Chicory can be eaten fresh, unblanched in small doses; but for cooking, the blanched hearts have a better flavour.

Cut off the heart or head just above the root, then remove a cone-shaped wedge from the centre of the base, allowing cooking heat to penetrate better and reducing the cooking time to preserve all the goodness.

After cutting, chicory should be stored in the dark. If stored in a covered container in the fridge it will keep about a week; but of course it is better if used fresh.

To eat it as a salad, cut the blanched head across thinly in slices, and add your favourite dressing or a few drops of lemon juice.

Here are a few simple recipes to start you experimenting.

Boiled or Steamed Chicory
Prepare the hearts as above. Cook in a stainless-steel saucepan if possible, and add just a little water and a few drops of lemon juice. Steam gently for about 10 minutes. Do not overcook.

Wash and trim the chicory. Melt 2 oz. butter in a heavy saucepan (stainless steel if possible), add 1½ lb. prepared chicory, juice of ½ a lemon, and salt and pepper. Now add 3 tablespoons of water, cover, and cook gently for 30 to 40 minutes, or until tender. Serve with cooking liquor.

Chicory with Cheese and Bacon

1 lb. chicory
1 tablespoon lemon juice
1½ tablespoons butter
2 tablespoons flour
½ pint cooking liquor plus milk
Salt and pepper
2 oz. grated cheese
4 tablespoons breadcrumbs
4 rashers of bacon, lightly cooked

Wash and trim the chicory, and boil in a little water with the lemon juice. Drain and keep the liquor. Melt butter and stir in the flour; remove from heat and stir in the ½ pint of liquid (made up of cooking liquor and milk). Bring to boil and stir for several minutes. Season with salt and pepper. Add the grated cheese and stir in till it melts. Then put chicory and bacon rashers in layers in an oven-proof dish, covering each layer with the sauce. Top with the breadcrumbs, dot with butter, and bake in a moderate oven until heated well through and brown on top (about 20 minutes).

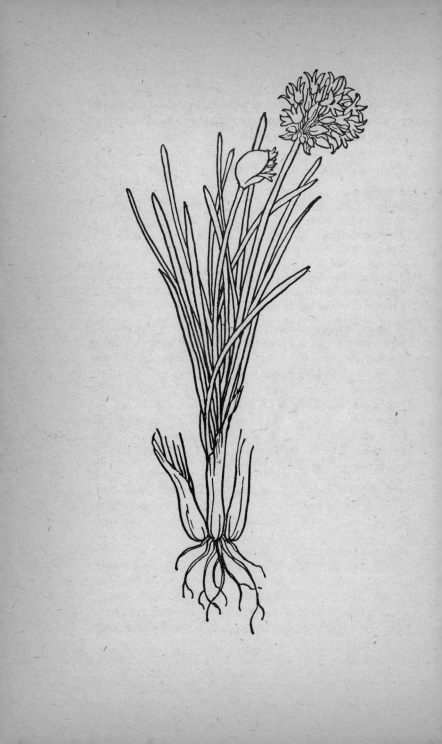

Chives

Allium schoenoprasum LILIACEAE

There is in every cook's opinion
No savoury dish without an onion;
But lest your kissing should be spoiled
The onion must be thoroughly boiled!

So said Jonathan Swift, and so at one time or another have all of us felt about the pungent smell of onions. This anti-social property is also shared by their small cousins, onion chives and garlic chives. But those of us who have any knowledge of natural medicine know that the onion family, with garlic at its head, is one of the greatest blessings to mankind in all the plant kingdom. I venture to say that if more people questioned their natureopathic physicians on the use of garlic in "miraculous" treatment of asthma and bronchitis, there would be an astonishing decrease in the misery caused by these diseases. Chest complaints cannot all be laid at the doorstep of smog and pollution. Some come from bad nutrition, causing imbalance and consequent bodily malfunction, which our foetid air only aggravates; and for most of these inherent bodily weaknesses garlic or one of its chive relatives can be of inestimable value.

I don't propose in this book to deal with garlic itself. The study of all its cleansing properties would fill a very much larger volume; but I hope to write at length of it in a further book.

Chives have, to a lesser degree, very similar properties in the safeguarding of general good health and the warding off of disease. They contain, amongst other valuable constituents, iron, pectin and sulphur, and are a mild natural antibiotic. They help to strengthen the stomach and combat high blood pressure, and have a tonic effect on the kidneys. Every invalid recuperating from serious illness should have chives every day in the diet, for they have a stimulating effect on the appetite and, like all herbal medicine, have no troublesome side-effects. Chives also reduce the indigestibility of fats in food—a boon to those cholesterol-level watchers.

The herb came to Europe via the Asian cultures, and it is mentioned in early Chinese herbal writings. Marco Polo is credited by some with spreading its fame anew around the Mediterranean.

Onion Chives is a grassy-leaved perennial, with round, hollow leaves and bright little pinkish-mauve pom-poms of flowers in the spring, summer, and sometimes even autumn. If you want the plant for decoration only, by all means let it flower, but keep a few clumps for culinary use, and nip off the flowers as they appear. The plant will grow better and bushier the more it is picked for use. Unfortunately, chives die right down during the really cold weather, although, with judicious autumn feeding, I have sometimes kept them growing right through a mild winter. Pick the very last green leaves in early winter and enjoy them, then put a stake beside the clump and watch for regrowth in early spring. The chives which "disappear" from a garden usually get dug up and damaged during deep digging or garden re-planning in winter. Put that stake in, tie a flag on it saying "Chives"; then, come the first warm weather, you can lift the newly shooting clump, divide it if you wish, and make either a decorative border or a family medicine chest for the coming season.

You can use chives on or in almost every savoury dish. When I serve out the meal each evening, my last stop before the dining-table is always the chives or parsley bed. Just chop up a few leaves and sprinkle on. If your spouse or your family objects to the aroma, chew a few parsley sprigs after eating chives. This will remove the after-effects. A few drops of aniseed oil on the tongue will do the same thing.

If you are a percolated-coffee drinker, tip the grounds on the chives bed. They seem to relish them. Well-fed soil is essential for chives, for the plants take nitrogen and potassium out of the ground. Grow comfrey near by if possible, and you will have huge, healthy chive plants. (Comfrey roots are a rich source of nitrogen in readily available form.) Yellowing of the tips of the spear-shaped leaves means the chives are underfed, and are crying out for nutriment.

Garlic Chives are a little different. Their leaves are strap-shaped, and they have a white, starry head of flowers. Their flavour is of true garlic, but in a much milder form. Again, use them raw, in salads, sauces and all savoury dishes. They have good antiseptic properties, and help to check the spread of contagious diseases when on the breath. Like garlic itself, they have a deterrent action on the T.B. bacillus, but are not harmful or injurious to the body in any way.

Garlic chives and roses seem to be companion plants. As well as increasing the perfume of the roses, the chives have a repellent effect on certain insects, notably aphis and when they are planted amongst roses the incidence of disease seems to be considerably less. One large rose nursery I know now gives plants of garlic chives with each order.

Use the herb freely; you cannot have too much of it. Use it wherever onion taste is required if this is too strong for you.

Chives can be quick-frozen very successfully if you need them right through the year; but, of course, some of their health-giving properties are lost in so doing. They can also be dried on screens, but tend to go yellow and lose their appetizing colour. Fresh chives grow so abundantly that you should have plenty for one household with only several plants.

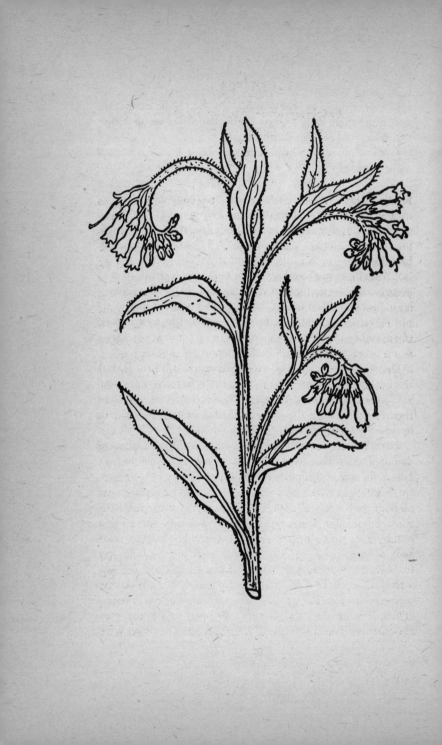

Comfrey

Symphytum officinale BORAGINACEAE

Russian comfrey and garlic could together, according to natural health usage, almost halve the present ills of western civilization. Here I am throwing down the gauntlet; but when I read of the amazing healing powers of comfrey in chest and bronchial troubles, its use in natural T.B. sanatoriums in Europe and Scandinavia, its success in the treatment of gastric and varicose ulcers, its external use in ointments for healing skin ulceration and tissue damage resulting from severe burns, acne, and other skin conditions, its value in many female disorders, and its bone and teeth-building powers in children, I am amazed that it is not growing in a position of honour in every garden. Its benefits are not confined to aiding the health of mankind and raising improved livestock; for its value is enormous to the home gardener in maintaining and increasing soil fertility, in breaking down the compost heap more quickly, and in adding its own rich stores of minerals to his garden.

The "miracle worker" in comfrey, for the rapid healing of damaged tissue both internally and externally, is a substance called allantoin. Allantoin has been found to be a cell-proliferant, a substance that speeds up the rate of natural replacement of body cells. This is important when body tissue has been damaged or injured in any way; but it is also important in a healthy body, to maintain the cell growth and replacement rate and to keep illnesses at bay. Comfrey taken internally acts through the bloodstream, where its natural calcium and B_{12} vitamins also get to work through the system. Then it's a case of "new cells for old", with comfrey waving the magic wand.

Comfrey has had the name "knit-bone" since the wise ancient physicians first learnt of its properties. The leaves were pulped, mixed with oil or wine (water tended to be suspect, even in those days), and applied externally to fractures as a healing poultice; the juice of leaves and roots was taken internally. There is an ever-growing list of reports of amazing recoveries in cases in which tissue damage has been prolonged and severe, as in tuberculosis. Comfrey is extensively used today in natural medicine, and I have proved its efficacy in my own family. We prefer to put one or two of the leaves through the juicer when making a vegetable cocktail (perhaps carrot and celery juice), so that it is used immediately in its fresh state. It can be cooked, the older leaves steamed like spinach and served with a drop or two of lemon juice. The young leaves can be eaten in a salad; but, like borage leaves, they are slightly hairy, and not to everyone's taste. I have found them quite palatable chopped into tiny pieces and sprinkled through a salad bowl (one or two leaves should be sufficient). Have some every day!

An old German recipe for comfrey is to fry in oil the small leaves dipped in a light batter. These look rather like flat, greenish fish when cooked, a talking-point perhaps for a dinner-party appetizer. Just cook them very quickly in the hot oil, drain, and serve immediately—or when they have cooled down if you wish.

The roots are a rich source of all comfrey's blessings. This is the part of the plant most used in ointments and salves, for it has slightly more potency. But unless you want to disturb and plunder the roots be content with the leaves. There is enough goodness there for any household.

Comfrey leaves can be put through the juice extractor and mixed with tomato juice or other vegetable juices. Two or three large mature leaves should be picked right from the base of their fleshy stems, and chopped coarsely. Add a little water, and put the mixture through the extractor once. Then collect the green stuff left in the basket, add a little more water, and put this through again. The gluey greenish-brown glumph pouring from the spout is now in an easily assimilable form to go to work in repairing and renewing body tissue. Remarkable results in the healing of scar tissue, particularly the incision scars of surgical operations, have been achieved with comfrey, taken internally and applied externally as well.

If a member of your family is unfortunate enough to suffer a sprain or any skin condition needing comfrey, the leaves can be applied direct to the skin on a bandage or as a poultice. One method of preparing the leaves for this purpose is to heat them in a little water (do not boil), then let them stand until luke-warm. Pulp the leaves (don't forget to drink the leftover juice) and apply the warm moist "green gold" to the injured spot. Then bandage as necessary. This treatment can be repeated as often as required. The cool mucilage of comfrey is soothing and healing and cannot possibly damage any sore or sensitive tissues.

The comfrey plant is a vigorously growing one. Its roots will forage deep down into the subsoil, dredging up the stores of minerals and nutrients often sadly lacking in depleted topsoil. It has been used by farmers to break up new heavy ground before planting foodcrops. After the foliage is ploughed in to decompose and provide rich nitrogen and calcium elements, the slowly rotting roots in their deep beds make drainage channels to allow air and moisture to penetrate. The only drawback is that comfrey is so keen to grow and be of service that any small pieces of root left in the soil will burst again into life and vigour. Surely it is no hardship to have amongst the new crops clumps of this herb, whose prodigality is equalled only by its manifold uses to mankind.

The abundant leaves can be used as a green manure, which is very easy to apply. Simply cut off the spent outside leaves from the clump, drop them around your plants and lightly chop them in with a spade or hoe. Their quick decomposition will free nitrogen and calcium into the topsoil.

Comfrey was placed by the astrologers under the dominion of Saturn, the sign of service in helping others—a very apt placing in the light of all the bounty it has to give. The large clumps will grow 3 to 4 feet high, and with a breadth of about 3 feet. The bright green leaves, growing to about 18 inches long, curve back towards the earth, and in spring several flowering stems will appear, bearing downward-drooping clusters of small, bell-shaped trumpets. The flowers on individual plants may be mauve, bluish, or even yellow, but most are a soft plum colour. Like all herbs, the plant grows better and stronger if not allowed to flower: so nip off the flowering stems unless you want them for seed. Sow the seeds in the early spring.

Once you have even one plant, you will never be without comfrey. A perennial, it can also be increased by lifting the clump (and a mature plant can be quite a lift) and dividing it into root pieces. This is best done in late summer. Set each piece of about 3 inches in length at a slight angle into the ground (or small pot, so you can plant out in the following spring), and cover to within about 1 inch from the top of the root. In the warmer weather, within a week or so new small leaves will be showing through. You can also chop off some of the outside offsets from the clump and transplant these, to avoid lifting the whole plant.

The leaves dry naturally to a brittle brown, and this is another herb not recommended for home-drying. However, the quick decomposing of the leaf and stem tissue can be helpful to gardeners: comfrey leaves are most beneficial additions to the compost heap. The chemical composition of the leaves is very close to that of animal manures, and breaking down in a very short time can help a bin of compost along in approximately half the usual 2 to 3 months' "cooking" time. My own bins, with the addition of comfrey, yarrow, tansy and valerian, are ready in about six weeks. The chapter on Soil Fertility gives the procedures for using these herbs in compost.

The home gardener seldom has to worry about the drought conditions that comfrey cannot stand—conditions that make large-scale plantings impracticable in country areas without irrigation. So use all the advantages of one or two comfrey plants in your backyard. Grasshoppers and caterpillars know what is good for them, too, and comfrey leaves are often their first stop in visiting the herb garden: so keep a constant vigil.

Give the plants sunshine and moisture, deeply dug soil, and a situation where their abundant growth will not encroach on more delicate plants, and they will give your family all the goodness with which nature has endowed them.

Dandelion

Taraxacum officinale COMPOSITAE

The common dandelion is probably the most underestimated and maligned "weed" ever to be consigned to the rubbish-heap. For generations, gardeners have complained about the plant's encroachment into the flower and vegetable domain, and the difficulty in completely eradicating the tenacious roots and prolific seed heads. Dandelions, in spite of them, keep coming up smiling and, for the good of our health, it is just as well they do! Just listen to a record of their virtues: They contain potassium and calcium salts, manganese, sodium, sulphur, vitamins A, B, C and D, and that necessary liver-regulating substance, choline. The plants will grow and prosper only near human habitation, and are found all over the world wherever man has pushed back indigenous trees, shrubs and grasses. In comes the "stirrer" (its botanical name comes from the Greek *taraxis*—to stir up), insistently reminding gardeners of its often unrecognized value.

> Star-disked dandelions, just as we see them
> lying in the grass like sparks that have
> leaped from the kindling sun of summer.

Oliver Wendell Holmes followed the lead of the ancient philosophers who placed dandelions under the dominion of the Sun. The leaves of the plants were used as a general spring tonic and blood purifier as soon as the first warm weather brought them into full growth. Their potency is greatest in spring and summer. During these seasons, the milky juice from the stems and leaves can be dropped carefully on to any warts on the skin. With repeated applications, the warts will soon blacken, shrivel, and drop off altogether.

The cleansing action of the herb is used to "stir up" the liver and gall, promoting their healthy functioning, and thereby ridding the body efficiently of wastes and poisons, as well as regulating a whole host of basic bodily functions. Dandelion tea has also been used in treatments for rheumatism, and has the reputation of freeing the liver and kidneys from stones, if used regularly in the diet. A spring tonic of dandelion leaf tea is said to inhibit the hepatitis virus, and undoubtedly a healthy liver is less likely to succumb than a sluggish overloaded one.

Dandelions need no description from me. Everyone knows their yellow flowers that close up tight when rain is soon due, their "clocks" of seeds and rosettes of leaves. Their name is Anglicized from the French *dent-de-lion*, referring to the backward-slanting toothed shape of the leaves. There are many variations in leaf characteristics. Some are darker green and slightly furry, with rounded teeth, some are brilliant green, less hardy in hot weather, with sharply-indented longer leaves, but all have much the same medicinal value.

The roots of the dandelion, dug in the second year of growth, can be roasted and used instead of coffee. Dig up the whole plant in the autumn. Cut off the leaves, and use in salads, or put through the juicer, or add to the compost heap where they are very welcome. Then wash and dry the large tap roots (rubbing off the small hair rootlets), and dry in a cool oven till quite brittle. Roast them to a light brown when needed and grind as coffee. One or two teaspoons brews a cup of pleasant flavour, which has none of the bad effects that over-indulgence in strong coffee can produce.

Another apt name for the dandelion came also from France, where *pisse-en-lit* was the unhappy outcome of a child's occasional gorging on dandelion leaves and flowers. Our "Wet-the-beds" has remained to damage the dandelion's reputation, and its more valuable qualities have been overlooked.

The commercial uses of dandelions have not yet been fully explored, but it has been found that the plants breathe out ethylene gas. This would seem to justify the gardener's criticism of dandelions as a pest, because ethylene inhibits the growth and height of nearby plants. However, ethylene is used extensively now in artificial ripening of fruit, so some canny orchardists are putting Nature to work for them by scattering dandelion seeds under their fruit-trees. The ethylene given off can aid in the early ripening of the crop.

That most concentrated and balanced food plant, alfalfa, has a natural affinity for dandelions, and if the yellow sunny buttons and "four o'clocks" are found growing in a field, it is certain that alfalfa will grow there to perfection.

So use Nature's free materials wherever you find them. Dandelions will grow under the most deprived, difficult conditions, in crannies along public footpaths, on railway embankments, on wasteland, even at rubbish dumps; but wherever they grow, they are still of great medicinal value to man. I have precious clumps growing at the side of my gravel driveway. The more I pick the leaves to use in salads and juice drinks, the more vigorously they grow. In midsummer I make up batches of Dandelion Beer, from an old Scottish recipe. Half the quantity can be tried first, as one pound weight of dandelions is quite a large amount to obtain at once. This recipe below makes nine or ten 30-ounce bottles.

Dandelion Beer

Pull up one pound weight of leaves and tap roots (not rootlets), wash well, add rind and juice of two lemons, then add two gallons of water. Boil for $\frac{1}{4}$ hour. Strain the liquid over 2 lb. raw sugar, add 2 oz. cream of tartar, and half an envelope of lager yeast. (The original recipe called for fresh yeast, $\frac{1}{4}$ of a cake, but the packaged yeast seems to make a better brew.) Let the liquid stand in stainless steel or porcelain bowls for three days, covering lightly. Never use aluminium vessels for making herb beers. Bottle in brown or dark green bottles, cork well, and it will be ready to drink in one week; but it will be even better if you leave it for two.

The beer is slightly bitter, more to be sipped than quaffed in one swallow, but most refreshing on a hot summer's day. You can feel it doing you good.

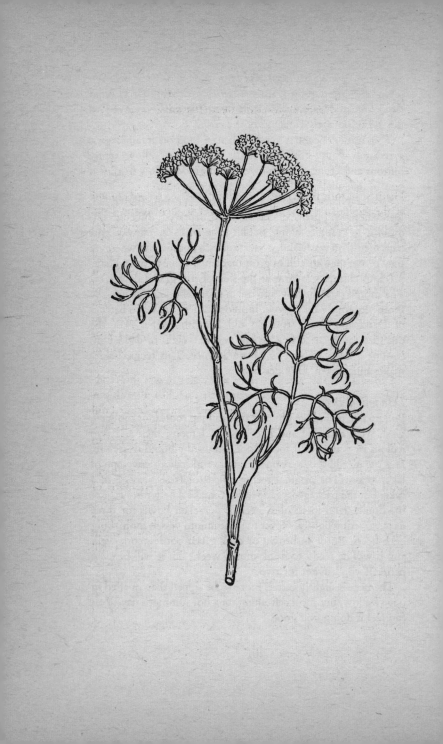

Dill

Anethum graveolens UMBELLIFERAE

The first historical references to dill go back to records found in the Egyptian tombs. Physicians used it then in the same manner and for the same purpose as we do now, as a powerful digestive aid.

The herb is an annual, and can be grown easily from seed sown right through from spring to autumn. In warm areas it can be sown all the year round. If you let one plant flower and set seed, you will find a few small seedlings around the area the following season. Like all the Umbelliferae (of which the carrot is a member), dill produces a prodigious quantity of seeds from each plant, and these are the part of the herb most commonly used therapeutically.

Dill-water is just as effective nowadays as it was in grand-mother's day, and is possibly even more useful to us with our richer foods and more artificial diet. Soak 1 oz. of bruised dill seeds in 1 pint of cold water for 6 hours, then sweeten to taste with honey. Give one tablespoon to adults, 1 teaspoon to children, to relieve indigestion.

The plant is very attractive, growing to about 3 feet high, with the typical lacy foliage and umbrella-shaped heads of gold flowers. There is a delicate bluish tint to the mature leaves, and when the seed is ripe, the leaves turn purple. Full sunshine suits it best, with plenty of water and good drainage. Do not grow it too close to fennel or angelica, for these relations will cross-pollinate and may lose their own individual flavours. Gather the seed heads when ripe (the seeds will be darkish mauve-brown, with lighter ribs), and store until needed in sealed glass jars. The usual method of separating the seeds from the stems is to rub the stalks with the hands inside a large plastic bag. Dill seed can keep its germinating power up to ten years, so one original plant can provide seeds to give you a constant supply for many years.

Dill contains potassium, sodium, sulphur and phosphorus, and has a very distinctive slightly metallic taste. The leaves are used, too, by Continental cooks, and are added to goulash and many fish and vegetable dishes, as well as being used to garnish hors-d'oeuvre and smorgasbord delicacies. Crab and lobster meat seem to me natural partners for dill's astringent flavour, and it helps, of course, in the digestion of the raw vegetables so often found in Scandinavian recipes.

Here are a couple of suggestions for cold platters:

Open Sandwich
Mash an avocado to purée, add some mayonnaise, chilli powder, a few drops of lemon juice, tomato quarters, black olive halves, sprigs of fresh dill. Blend loosely, and serve on lettuce on rye bread.

Pepper with Dill
Seed and wash half of a small red or green pepper. Fill with a mixture of cottage cheese blended with chopped dill, diced black olives and diced cucumber, the whole bound together with a little sour cream. Garnish with watercress or garden cress.

Dill Sauce
Here is a seventeenth century recipe. A modern bouillon cube can be added if stock is not available.

1½ tablespoons butter
1½ tablespoons flour (wholemeal if possible)
1½ cups stock
2 tablespoons chopped dill
½ tablespoon lemon juice
½ tablespoon sugar, raw
1 egg yolk
Salt and pepper

Melt the butter, blend in the flour, and add the hot stock gradually, blending constantly to keep smooth. Add all the other ingredients except the egg yolk. Keep this aside until the sauce is slightly cooled (to avoid curdling) then add the yolk, and whisk again. This is a delicious sauce for beef.

Cucumber Sauce

1 large fresh cucumber
1 oz. oil or butter
1 oz. flour (wholemeal)
1 tablespoon chopped dill
1 cup sour cream
2 cups stock or 1 bouillon cube dissolved in 2 cups of water

Peel the cucumber, remove the seeds and chop it into dice, then melt the butter or put the oil in a pan, and add the flour, stirring well. Add the stock or bouillon, then the diced cucumber, a small pinch of sugar and a drop of lemon juice. Simmer slowly for about 10 to 15 minutes. Add the chopped dill and the sour cream just before serving, and reheat quickly.

Seafood Salad

Cook 2 cups of long-grain rice in plenty of salted water, till the grains are fluffy and plump. Wash with cold water to separate the grains, and allow to cool and drain completely. Place the rice in a bowl and add the following: a small tin crabmeat chunks, 1 red and 1 green pepper, chopped, a little sliced celery, several good-sized leaves of fresh dill, chopped, and toss with ¾ cup of good mayonnaise to which salt and ½ tablespoon of lemon juice have been added. Chill well before serving, piling into a mound in the centre of the serving platter, and garnish with fresh whole dill sprigs.

Shrimp Moulds with Dill

1 small can tomato juice
1 oz gelatine
1½ cups shrimps (or prawns)

Juice of half a lemon
Dash of cayenne
Several chopped gherkins
Sprigs of fresh dill
Tablespoon of chopped green pepper

Soften the gelatine in a little cool water, then heat gently to dissolve. Gradually stir in the tomato juice, then all the remaining ingredients. Leave the mixture cool until nearly set (otherwise all the shrimps will sink to the bottom of the mould), then spoon into individual moulds. When set, turn out onto a bed of cucumber slices and garnish with more sprigs of dill and a few of the shrimps.

Spinach with Dill

In Elizabethan England, Henry Butte, a gourmet and scholar, experimented with flavour companions for dill. Here is one of his ideas:

Before cooking spinach, add a good handful of chopped dill to the leaves. Slice several shallots, green tops as well, and add these also. Then boil or steam the spinach mixture as usual. Try this served with a dob of butter on top and a trickle of lemon juice.

Dill is indigenous to the Mediterranean, and Southern Russia and Scandinavia, and is a very ancient herb. It was used often in the incantations and magic rites associated with protection from witchcraft. On St John's Eve (23rd June) various herbs were smoked or dried in the holy fires lit to mark the festival period. These herbs were then taken back by the people to their homes, and hung there as protection from sorcerers, witches and the Evil Eye. Vervain, hypericum and yarrow were also used.

Many writers recommend sowing dill seed where the plants are to remain, for the herb can be difficult to transplant. I have never found it so. My own nursery pots of dill are all transplanted from seed boxes or punnets, and with ordinary care they will transplant once again to the garden without any casualties. Although the seed can be sown almost all the year, spring is the best time, because the plants will grow quickly during the hot weather to come.

Plant dill beside your cabbage patch in the vegetable garden. It helps the growth of carrot plants, too, but be sure to dig out the dill or, use it before it flowers: *in bloom* it can inhibit the growth of the carrots, owing to chemical changes in the plant at that time. All these "companion plant" relationships can be traced to chemicals either taken or supplied by one plant with benefit to another. This field seems to me of increasing importance in its applications. Overcropped or depleted land could perhaps be brought back under cultivation earlier if we were able to use the gradually growing knowledge coming in from all parts of the world. Plants have interlocking economies just as important to them as our trade agreements are to us. "Reciprocal business" seems a wonderfully waste-free way of using these chemical-swopping activities, without having to add unnatural outside agents.

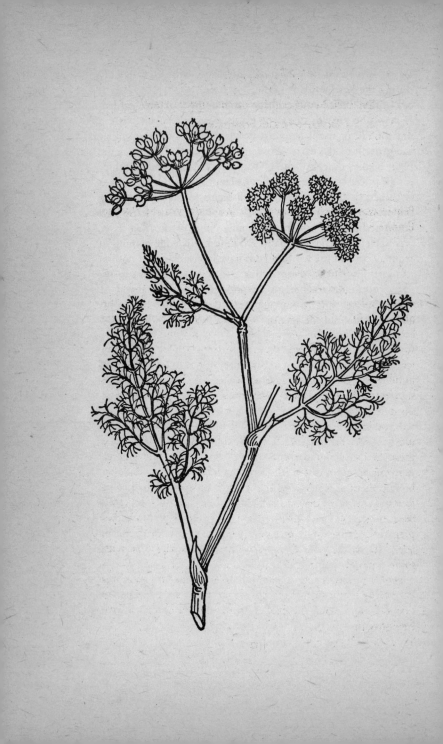

Fennel

Sweet Fennel *Foeniculum vulgare* UMBELLIFERAE

Florence Fennel *Foeniculum dulce*

Fennel was a much favoured herb in the days of the Roman Empire.

> *So gladiators fierce and rude*
> *Mingled it with their daily food,*
> *And he who battled and subdued*
> *A wreath of Fennel wore.*

Longfellow does not say just how the fennel kept the gladiators fit and trim, but we now know that it has a definite action in predigesting and breaking down oily and fatty food-stuffs in the diet. Indeed, Roman matrons also drank fennel tea, and used it when cooking fatty food, not to perform feats in the arena, but to keep their waistlines trim and their figures supple and healthy Fennel owes most of its popularity to its slimming qualities.

Another, and also very important property of fennel, is its use in eye afflictions. Together with rue (see p. 163), it is prescribed as an eye strengthener and restorer of failing sight. A strong solution of fennel, using the leaves only, is made by boiling them in water until the water is reduced by half. This lotion is applied to the eyes each day, when it is cool. Repeated use is necessary. Exact quantities are not really critical in herbal preparations. The body uses only what it requires of the herb, and discards the rest. There is no harmful build-up as with some types of synthetic drugs.

Fennel produces such a multitude of seed that it naturalizes very easily in one or two seasons. Wild fennel does degenerate gradually in flavour, but makes up for this by hardier insect-free growth.

Garden, or sweet fennel, is a perennial, a tall rampant-growing plant some 3 to 4 feet in height. It closely resembles dill in appearance, and the two should never be sown close together: they will cross-pollinate and their flavours intermingle and deteriorate. Fennel is best planted on its own, in calcium-rich soil, away from the formal herb beds, in a spot where its gangling leggy growth will not overpower other plants, and with space all around it, not cramped by shrubs or trees. It thrives best in rather rocky, sandy soils, being undemanding of extra feeding. Overfeeding can make the herb more susceptible to aphis attack, and to young snails, which find shelter in the leaf stem junctions. Plentiful water in the early stages is essential. After this period, ordinary watering should suffice. The plant may need staking or tying if exposed to strong winds.

Harvest the seeds when they turn from green and plump to brown and dry, and save them for pickles, chutneys and flavouring borsch soup. You can also do as our grandparents did; chew fennel seed to allay hunger pangs. The seeds were often carried to church and prayer-meetings; and when little Willie's stomach started to rumble during the sermon, fennel seeds were an unobtrusive way of damping down his need for Sunday dinner. So gain a twofold benefit from fennel: if you want to slim, chew some of the seeds not with but instead of lunch.

Leaves of fennel are sometimes placed on the bottom of the pan when baking bread in Italy. A few seeds sprinkled on the top of pastries or bread rolls before cooking give a delicate aniseed flavour and a delectable aroma.

A traditional recipe for fennel is to use it with any oily fish, as in the following recipe. Fennel grows naturally near the seashore round the Mediterranean, once again showing Nature's provision for counteracting the disadvantages of one food by ensuring its opposite or complementary ingredient is near by.

Whole Fish with Fennel
Clean and scale the fish, leaving on the head and tail. Then

make a marinade of oil, vinegar, and chopped fennel (use the leaves and a couple of stems), and steep the fish in this for about one hour. Place the fish then on a shallow cook-and-serve platter. Blanch several stalks of fennel until they will bend easily. (Dip them in water close to the boil, but not boiling.) Wrap these around the body of the fish; fasten with toothpicks if necessary. Then cook the fish in a moderate oven until the flesh is tender, basting with a knob of butter when necessary. Serve it straight from the oven, with the fennel still in place. Garnish with tiny boiled or steamed potatoes, and chopped fennel leaves sprinkled over.

This fennel butter to glaze fish or vegetables is very appetising too: Chop sprigs of fennel leaves, and mix with two tablespoons of butter, and vegetable salt to taste. Blend well, and drop in little balls on the fish or vegetable dish.

Fennel should *not* be grown anywhere near the vegetable garden. It will inhibit the growth and fruiting of tomato plants. Coriander should not be grown near fennel either: seed formation of both plants will be poor. If you have a dog, "Plant fennel near the kennel." It will help to keep fleas away, for they are repelled by its scent.

There is an annual variety of fennel, Florence Fennel, or Finocchio. This is a much shorter, less straggly plant, which as it matures swells out at the base to form a thickened stem about 4 to 6 inches across.

Cut off the whole plant just above the root, and trim off the foliage and top part of the stem, leaving a plump juicy vegetable about 6 to 8 inches long, ready to slice into your salad bowl, or steam and serve hot, drizzled over with a knob of butter.

You can slice it very thin diagonally, dress it lightly with oil and lemon juice, and serve it as a salad on its own; you can also sauté the thin slices quickly in oil or butter, and serve on wedges of toast or with other vegetables.

Use finocchio in egg dishes and hors d'oeuvres too. This unusual omelette is a meal in itself, or a light first course, depending only on the size of the helping.

Florence Fennel Omelette

1 root Florence Fennel
Shallots, lettuce leaves
1 tablespoon red capsicum
1 tablespoon olive oil
1 crushed garlic clove
3 tablespoons milk
2 well-beaten eggs
1 tablespoon wholemeal flour

Heat the oil, lightly fry the shallots, fennel, lettuce leaves, and capsicum, add the crushed garlic clove, and cook over low heat for about 5 minutes. Add the milk, and simmer a further 5 minutes, covering the pan. Then add the beaten eggs mixed with the flour, raise the heat slightly, and cook gently until the eggs are set. Cut the omelette in half, turn it upside down, and serve immediately with lemon wedges. The whole thing is best done in a traditional heavy omelette pan, but any heavy wide utensil will do.

Finocchi Siciliana

In Sicily, "Finocchi Siciliana" presents Florence fennel in a more subtle nest of flavour.

4 or 5 Florence fennel roots
4 tablespoons olive oil
1 small onion, chopped
Salt and freshly-ground black pepper
1 cup chicken broth
Parmesan cheese

Wash and drain the fennel roots, then cut them into sections lengthwise. In a heavy pan, sauté the fennel in the hot oil for about 10 minutes, shaking the pan often to prevent it catching. Add the broth and seasonings, cover and simmer slowly until the fennel is tender. Sprinkle the cheese over the top and brown under a hot griller for several minutes before serving.

Sweet fennel was used in ancient fertility rites, where its quick and prolific germination was part of the ritual. It was also one of the strewing herbs, used to cover cold stone and earth floors when carpets were only in the castles of kings and their noblemen. One Italian family told me that fennel is included in bouquets presented to young couples when entering their new home, symbolizing protection from fire, evil and accidents. It was one of the old "Witches' Herbs", used not by them but against them.

In pastures, fennel is grown to increase the milk yield of dairy cattle and goats, and is still used as a food supplement given at calving time.

Scented-leafed Geraniums

GERANIACEAE

Recent experiments in the study of plant perfumes have shown that molecules of the plant's substance are present in the perfume exhaled by the flowers or leaves. So sniffing a perfumed flower can be not only pleasant but therapeutic as well. The scented nosegays and posies of eighteenth- and nineteenth-century ladies could well have given them some protection from air-borne germs as well as sensory pleasure. Even the men, walking the sometimes fetid and certainly unsanitary streets of the cities, carried small bunches of aromatic herbs and spices to help disguise the rank infective air. The use of snuff was a refinement of this practice, the herbs and spices used being powdered and inhaled; and the sneezing that followed cleared the breathing passages. Many of the common ingredients of snuff have been found, through later scientific research, to have a real antiseptic action, cinnamon and marjoram being two of the strongest. Instead of that cigarette, why not start a "new" fad? Produce a tiny snuff-box from your vest pocket, take two elegant sniffs, and free into your jaded sinuses some of Nature's natural antiseptic aromatic herbs and spices.

The leaves of scented geraniums, bruised and used as a poultice applied to cuts and grazes were often mentioned in the old herbals. They have quite pronounced antiseptic properties.

The original geranium was the single scarlet "Herb Robert" or Cranesbill from *geranus*, a crane. The flower shape was said to resemble the head of this bird. This small-flowered geranium would not recognize some of the impressive large double and scented-leaved members of its family which have been hybridized for garden display. Most of the scented so-called "geraniums" are pelargoniums, and there are several very worthy of

115

a place in your herb garden or border. Dry them for pot-pourri (see p. 31) hung head downwards in small bunches, or laid flat on screens.

They do have various culinary uses, too, which are decorative as well as unusual. Try several perfect leaves of the lemon- or rose-scented variety bruised gently with the fingers to release their fragrance, in individual glass or crystal finger bowls for a very special dinner or reception. Place pats of butter on a bed of the leaves. For everyday use, put a leaf of the peppermint, lemon, rose or lime geranium on the bottom of the greased pan before baking a wholemeal teacake or a tray of muffins. Add one or two leaves to jellies and milk puddings. Egg custard can benefit too. Crush a large handful of the leaves, place them in the bath, run the hot tap first, swishing the leaves about in the water, then add the cold water, and yourself.

Geranium leaves can be used very effectively in flower arranging too. They harmonize well with formal blooms like rose-buds, gladioli florets and flowering bulbs. Add them to a float bowl of pansies, or any beautiful but unscented flower. Bruise the leaves, so that they can release their perfume.

Insect pests do not relish the strongly scented geranium leaves, and will not attack them, so give these plants plenty of your allotted garden space for herbs, and put some in the border or street planting strip, too. Rockeries and sunny corners suit them well, and you will soon have thick healthy clumps. The flowers are all rather inconspicuous, the main value of the plant being in its hardiness and ground-covering ability, together with its perfume, of course.

The scented geraniums are all hardy perennials and will grow easily and quickly from stem cuttings with a "heel" of old wood, and I have taken these as late as May with good results. All the varieties mentioned will withstand heat and dryness, and can be used as street or footpath plantings where other less hardy herbs might fail. They can also be increased by layering (see p. 23); but they grow so easily from cuttings that striking these is a sure-fire way to gain a good stock of new plants to give away come Christmas, or to swop with gardening friends.

Rose-scented Geranium *Pelargonium graveolens*

A beautifully-formed plant, with a semi-trailing low-growing habit, and a slight orange cast on some of the leaves. The most delicious perfume, and a quick grower.

Lemon-scented Geranium *Pelargonium limonium*

Large deeply cut leaves with a strong perfume, growing into a big bush which can reach 5 or 6 feet in height unless cut back hard occasionally to keep it within bounds. The tiny pinkish-mauve flowers appear in the spring. There is also a lemon-scented variety called *Pelargonium crispum variegata*, with a compact low habit of growth and tiny curly green leaves. paler yellowish-green at the top of each stem.

Peppermint Geranium *Pelargonium tomentosum*

A delightfully soft velvety plant with ivy-shaped leaves and inconspicuous white flowers. It is a low grower, tending to trail about, and likes a little less sun than the others. Very easy to propagate from cuttings.

Coconut Geranium *Pelargonium enossularoides*

Dark green rosettes of leaves from which come long horizontal sprays of deep pink flowers in spring and summer. These flowering stems lie along the soil, and where they touch, a new rosette of leaves forms to start off another plant. Soon you will have a very big patch of geranium unless you dig up the new plants and put them elsewhere. It is ideal for quickly covering banks or nature strips, and very hardy. Full sunshine and plenty of water when the flowering stems are spent will ensure better coverage by the new plants. The scent is of true coconut, slightly bitter, and should not be added to pot-pourri.

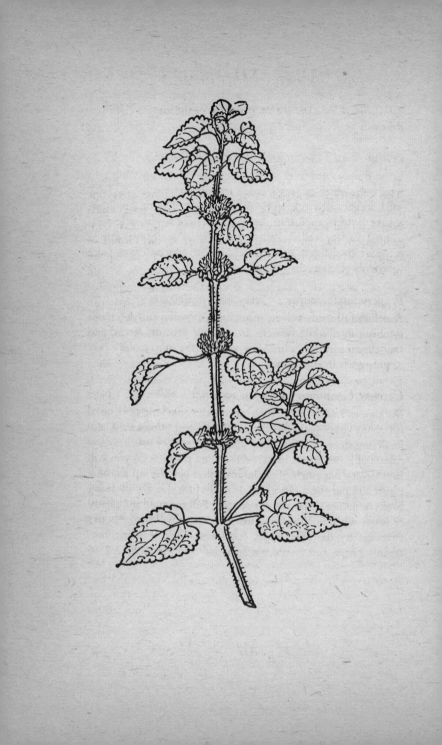

White Horehound

Marrubium vulgare LABIATAE

This is one herb which has proved invaluable to me. Everyone knows the prickly sensation in throat and nasal areas which heralds an old-fashioned, heavy cold. I have proved to my own satisfaction, over and over again, that 8 or 10 small leaves of horehound, crushed and eaten slowly mixed with a tablespoon of honey to counter their very bitter taste, can stop a cold before it really starts if taken as soon as the first uncomfortable "cold feeling" is noticed, within the hour if possible. You can repeat the treatment again several times during the day to be doubly sure if you wish; it will not do you any harm, and the natural vitamin C will most certainly do you good.

I must admit this sounded too good to be true to me when I read repeatedly in old (and newer) herbal writings, "fresh leaves of horehound will ward off colds". However, I have proved it so often now that I no longer doubt the skill and knowledge of the first herbalist to discover its uses to man, and to prescribe it for colds and chest complaints. Plant minerals and vitamins are easily assimilable into the human body, and quickly go to work against that unnatural state called "illness".

Horehound has been prescribed for many generations for chest, nasal and sinus congestion, and was often an ingredient in snuff, a social habit that should be revived for its healthy protective cleansing of the nasal area.

The popularity of horehound beer for sufferers from any of these conditions has carried down from the Middle Ages to our own day. One large commercial group I know of markets many thousands of bottles of horehound beer yearly. Here are two recipes for making it, the first English, the second Australian:

Horehound Beer 1

To a large handful of leaves and stems add 3 gallons of water and 2 lb. of treacle. Boil for an hour, then strain and cool to blood heat. Add 2 tablespoons of yeast, and let stand for 24 hours covered with a clean cloth, then bottle. Ready to drink in one week.

Horehound Beer 2

Boil in a large saucepan gently for a half hour 2 oz. of fresh horehound leaves and stems and 1 oz. of fresh bruised ginger. Add 1 lb. raw sugar and sufficient boiling water to make one gallon in all. Let cool slightly. Add $\frac{1}{4}$ oz. tartaric acid and the juice of 1 lemon, and colour with a little burnt sugar (or a teaspoon of molasses). Add 2 tablespoons of fresh yeast when quite cool. Strain and let stand covered for two or three days. Bottle in dark brown or green bottles and seal tightly. Ready in two to three weeks.

I have also come by a recipe for horehound candy, a traditional simple "cough-lolly" which grandma used to make:

Horehound Candy

2 oz. fresh horehound
1½ cups water
1¾ lb. brown sugar
¼ cup corn syrup

Cook the horehound slowly in water for 15 minutes, if possible in a stainless steel or heavy saucepan with the lid on. Then let stand for one hour. Remove the horehound (tip it on the compost heap), then add the sugar and syrup to the liquid and boil to "hard-crack" stage (300 degrees F. on a candy thermometer). Pour into a greased shallow pan, and mark into squares.

The botanical name comes from the Hebrew *marrob*, a bitter juice, and the herb is certainly not a pleasant-tasting one in its raw state. It is a native of Europe, North Africa and Central Asia, and has naturalized in many parts of the world including Britain and North America, where in some states it is a declared noxious weed! How true is that definition of a weed "a plant whose uses to man have not yet been appreciated"!

The plant is ungainly and perhaps even untidy, the white downy stems and woolly leaves trailing along in all directions. In summer white whorls of flowers appear at the leaf axils, but these, too, are neither attractive nor showy. If ever an ugly duckling had a hidden swanlike soul it is horehound. It grows best in poor soil; my own horehound plants have the rockiest, most difficult corner in the garden.

Check with your Department of Agriculture before starting off a paddock of horehound to cure the world's ills. In your area it may be a declared weed.

Bill Wannan, in his entertaining book *Folk Medicine*, tells of horehound's role in the early Australian goldrush days. In the 1890s at Kalgoorlie, Chinese (clever, as always) who had come to work as cheap labour on the goldfields went away somewhat richer because of their knowledge of vitamin-rich horehound. The dried leaves were sold at steadily inflating prices to miners to brew a tonic tea. Old-timers swore by its efficacy. Horehound poultices were often used as a remedy for the "Barcoo rot", a skin disease caused by over-exposure to the dry heat of the inland together with vitamin deficiencies in the diet. The herb's reputation grew as one boundary rider passed on the good word to the next. Barcoo rot is seldom encountered now that more is known about diet, but horehound's praises are still sung on many outback stations by those old enough to remember.

Sow seeds of horehound in early spring. It is rather erratic in its germination. One seedling can be ready to transfer to its permanent home long before its neighbour has more than a single tiny leaf through the soil.

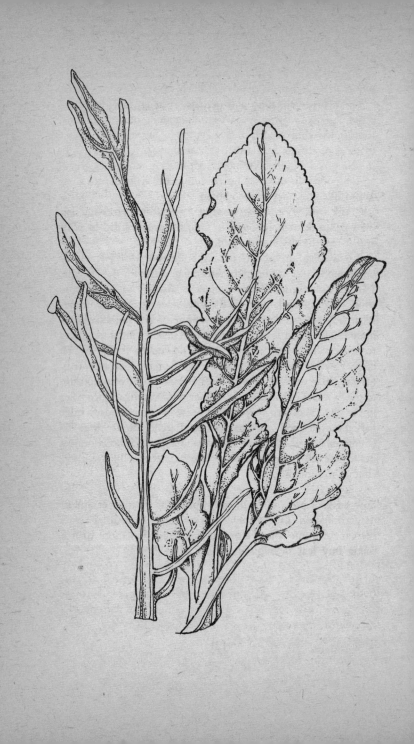

Horseradish

Cochlearia armoracia CRUCIFERAE

Authorities differ as to the correct botanical name for this herb; some of the confusion seems due to its variation in leaf shape and habit of growth, the *Encyclopaedia Britannica* referring to it as *Armoracia rusticana*, but Culpeper, and many later writers such as Clare Loewenfeld, who has the famous Chiltern Herb Nursery in Surrey, England, call it *Cochlearia armoracia*. It is even more confusing when it is occasionally called "Scurvy Grass", which is another plant altogether (*Cochlearia officinalis*), but as far as I can discover all the names refer to the same old pungent horseradish we serve with the roast beef.

The plant is a native of the muddy swamps near the seaside in Mediterranean areas, and it likes a cool, moist situation with deeply dug soil, free from stones or other rubbish, so that the tap root, the important part of the plant, can grow down deep and strong, unimpeded in its search for nourishment. Before planting, dig at least 2 feet down into the ground, loosening packed clay or subsoil as you go, and if you are a perfectionist you may want to sieve the soil, removing hard lumps or dead roots.

If the subsoil is too heavy, mix some coarse sand in with it before returning it to the hole, together with compost, and a few handfuls of blood and bone about a foot below the surface. Plant your horseradish seedling with its stem base about an inch below the soil surface and keep it well watered during its growth. The leaves as they grow have several different shapes, varying from plant to plant. Some are deeply toothed and rather stiff, others resemble spinach but are a paler green, and still others have almost no leaf stem at all, seeming to come straight from the root stock.

Snails love horseradish, and they will strip the leaves to skeletons unless a lookout is constantly kept.

The roots should be dug at the end of the first growing season, and the thick tap root separated from the others. Scrub it, and cut it into strips about $\frac{1}{4}$ inch wide to facilitate drying. It can then be dried on a tray in a cool oven (watch this carefully to avoid overheating or roasting). When completely dry, the root slivers will be quite brittle, and will snap when bent. Store these strips in a glass jar lined with tissue paper, and grate when needed.

The smaller root pieces can be cut into 3- or 4-inch lengths and replanted with the top about an inch below the soil surface. Rub off all but one strong shoot when regrowth begins, to give you only one crown and a single unbranched root. The herb needs plenty of water at all stages of its growth to keep the root fleshy and prevent any woodiness.

If you do not wish to dry the roots, store them after washing in white wine vinegar. They can be grated as required. Do not use cider vinegar for this; it will discolour the roots to a dark brown.

Horseradish is very effective in the treatment of sinus and antrum congestion. Taken internally in concentrated form, it helps to purify the bloodstream and rid the body of mucous wastes. It is a seasoning that can be used safely by diabetics. It is also a valuable addition to a dog's diet. The leaf, chopped small, helps to rid the animal of worms and build up the general body tone.

If you have a tendency to sinus congestion, add horseradish freely to your diet. There are many appetizing ways of using it in sauces and dressings for meat and vegetable dishes.

Almond Horseradish Sauce

2 tablespoons grated horseradish
1 oz. skinned almonds, chopped
1 oz. butter
1 cup cold milk

1 oz. wholemeal flour
1 teaspoon raw sugar
Seasoning to taste

Make a white sauce with the butter, flour and milk, boiling until thickened. Add the other ingredients. Heat through and serve at once with boiled beef or a dish of whole steamed vegetables.

Cold Horseradish Sauce

4 tablespoons grated horseradish
Pinch of paprika
2 teaspoons dry mustard
1 teaspoon wine vinegar
4 tablespoons yoghurt or thick cream

Mix first four ingredients together, then add the yoghurt or cream. Blend till creamy and smooth. Serve with a salad, cold meat or smorgasbord platter of vegetables.

It has been discovered recently that a clump of horseradish at each end of the potato rows can improve the health and resistance to disease of the potato tubers. This is another old farmer's tale that has been confirmed by controlled experiments in testing plots, both in Britain and the United States. Organic gardeners are ever seeking natural methods of improving crops and maintaining the fertility of the soil. It seems horseradish can give plants as well as humans the benefit of its natural antibiotic properties.

One word of warning: don't plant horseradish among the flower beds or the herbaceous border. Each piece of root broken off when digging will start another plant, and you will find yourself eliminating horseradish unto the third and fourth generation. Give it a spot at the far end of the garden where it can grow and multiply freely.

Hyssop

Hyssopus officinalis LABIATAE

Herbal writers don't agree on whether the biblical *èzob* is in fact *Hyssopus officinalis*. Some believe that it is a variety of savory (*Satureia thymus*), which was a native of the area and whose properties are very similar to those mentioned in the scriptures, but by far the greater number agree that although *Hyssopus officinalis* was not a native of Palestine it grew freely in Southern Europe and Asia, naturalizing as it went; and it could conceivably have been well established in Palestine by this time. Its properties are the same today as those mentioned in many parts of both the Old and New Testament. After reading one modern report in *Nature's Medicines*, by Richard Lucas,* I incline towards the second view. Medical doctors have always regarded the "cleansing" properties of hyssop as so much superstitution; but recent analysis has found that the mould that produces penicillin grows on the leaves of *Hyssopus officinalis*. So when lepers were forced to cleanse themselves ritualistically with hyssop before being allowed contact with their healthier kin, compassionate Nature provided a very suitable protection for parents and relatives, a powerful antibiotic.

The herb is a hardy perennial, a compact plant very like a large nemesia in its foliage, and with attractive blue flowers growing along one side of the flowering stems. It grows easily from seed, which should be sown in spring, and the new seedlings come through very quickly. Three or four days should see their two seedleaves through the soil. The clump as it grows can be divided with the spade if new plants are required. Hyssop needs sunshine. Its other demands are few, but it must have the sun to produce its flowers, which will then

* Wiltshire Book Co., New York, 1970.

bring the bees and the butterflies. Cabbage butterflies can be lured away from the cabbage patch if a few hyssop plants are at the other end of the garden in flower. So here is another common-sense bit of natural pest control.

A strong tea made from the leaves and flowering tops of hyssop is used in lung, nose and throat congestion and catarrhal complaints; and externally it can be applied to bruises to reduce the swelling and discoloration.

In England an old country remedy for wounds or cuts suffered working in the fields was to apply a poultice of the bruised leaves mixed with sugar. The risk of tetanus and other infections with these often deep cuts was high, because of the manures and perhaps rusty implements with which the farmers always worked. So once again, Nature's simple protection was called for. A black eye is another embarrassing affliction that hyssop can alleviate. Put a small bunch of the herb in a muslin or small nylon bag or twist of material, immerse in boiling water for a minute, then place on the eye as hot as is bearable. Repeat until the swelling and discoloration subside.

Several leaves of hyssop can be used to flavour soups and stews. It is a herb that will stand a longer cooking time, although it is still better to add it in the last quarter hour. The flavour of hyssop will blend well in a vegetable medley.

Vegetable Hotpot

½ stick celery
4 medium carrots
2 small onions
Chopped cabbage
Mustard or cress sprouts
4 tablespoons oil
1 cup stock
2 tablespoons cornflour
Small handful hyssop leaves
Salt and cayenne pepper

Wash and dice all the vegetables (except the sprouts), and add to the hot oil, tossing to coat them evenly. Sauté over moderate heat for several minutes. Add the hyssop and seasonings, then add the stock, cover and cook over medium heat for about 5 minutes. Add the sprouts just at the last minute, heat through and serve immediately. Do not overcook, as the vegetables should be crisp and chewy.

It is frequently used in the perfume industry, its concentrated oils being blended with other fragrances in eau-de-Cologne.

Plant hyssop as a low hedge around the vegetable patch. Its flowers will bring the bees, and its roots have been found to cleanse the soil and keep many soil pests at bay. Don't, however, grow it near radishes: the two plants are not compatible, and the radishes will have poor flavour.

Hyssop has also been found to improve the yield from grapevines if planted along the rows, particularly if the terrain is rocky or sandy, and the soil not as easy to work as it might be. So add another plant to the list of those that can improve the health and productivity of food crops. Some day soon, as man's distrust of artificial growing methods forces him to turn back to Nature, all these green natural "chemical factories" will once again be given the opportunity to work for us.

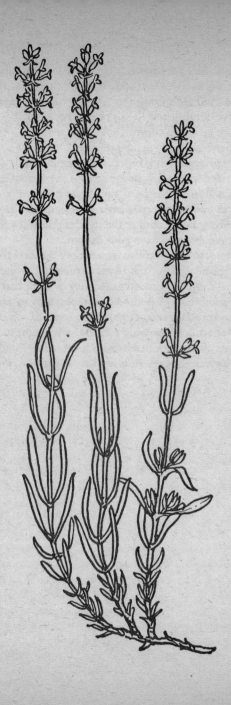

Lavender

English Lavender *Lavandula spica* LABIATAE
French Lavender *Lavandula stoechas*

Lavender and gentle old ladies seem fated to be associated. Many of us can remember the little bags of pink or lilac net, tied with velvet and satin ribbons, with which a maiden-aunt would honour the birthdays of her young nieces. Many a "hope chest" had little sachets of lavender amongst the linens and fine lawns, and the fragrance of this pleasant herb lasted through the years of girlhood till womanhood and marriage. The perfume of lavender is the longest-lasting of any herb in its dried state, and for this reason alone it is worth having a bush or two in your garden.

But its other uses, often little known, are more important. Lavender oil, extracted by distillation, is a very powerful antiseptic, and was used extensively during the last war, when surgical supplies were scarce and precious. In field hospitals and emergency aid stations, the herbs gathered from thousands of British gardens at the urgent request of desperate medical authorities, were once again used as of old in combating infection and cleansing and purifying surgical dressings and wards. Plant properties remain the same today as they were in the earliest epochs of the world's history. There is not a new variety of herb out each year with a blare of publicity. The needs of man and animals in illness have not changed much either, so plant remedies remain as effective as ever they were.

English Lavender is the variety from which the strongest oil is obtained. As a girl, I was told the Mitcham Lavender products were the best; and on recent inquiry I found that the old plantations of lavender at Mitcham, in Surrey (now unfortunately entirely built over by housing settlements) produced not only good quality oil, but a product priced six times higher than the French oil on the world market.

The chalky soils of Surrey provided lavender with one of its requirements, alkaline conditions. In this country, it is necessary to put plenty of dolomite or lime into the soil in preparation for planting a lavender bush. Work one or two handfuls well into the soil under the roots, and also sprinkle it through the topsoil around the plant, forking it in lightly. Lavender bushes will last and thrive if given this alkaline environment and plenty of water, with good drainage away from the roots.

My own French Lavender bushes remain vigorously growing and in flower for the greater part of the year. They live close to a rather decrepit piece of down-piping, which overflows at every heavy rain. Drainage is rapid, though, and the lavender bushes are fit and well, and covered with the long-stemmed spikes.

Plant a bush near your laundry door and, on a sunny still day, dry your prettiest handkerchiefs and underclothes spread out on the bush. English lavender is a compact, low-growing shrub, with long-stemmed heads of loosely-set deep-mauve flowers. The stems and silvery foliage are also used in the extraction of the oil. The flowers can be dried very easily if picked when the sun has evaporated any dew, and hung in small bunches head downwards for a couple of weeks. Humid weather will, of course, mean a longer drying time.

French Lavender grows to a hardy 3 to 4 feet high, with strong woody branches topped with short-stemmed soft mauve flower-heads above the greyish-green foliage. This variety is also very easy to dry.

Put equal quantities of bruised fresh lavender flowers and sugar in a glass jar. Seal, and shake well every few days. After about one month, sift the sugar to remove the lavender flowers, and you have a delicately perfumed topping for a cake or biscuits. Ice-cream made with lavender sugar is unusual and refreshing. Serve it decorated with one or two lavender flowers. Remember, before making your lavender sugar, the flowers must always be bruised first to release their perfumed oils. A small glass mortar and pestle, obtainable from chemical suppliers, is ideal for use with herbs. Small quantities may be crushed to make herbal oils or vinegars, and the glass will not retain individual odours and flavours as wood or stoneware may do.

Lavender oil is a powerful insect repellent. A few drops rubbed on the skin before bushwalking or barbecuing will repel troublesome midges, flies and mosquitoes. It can also be used for rubbing rheumatic joints and aches and pains due to over-exertion.

Italian Lavender is a delicate little member of the family, with small silvery leaves and the typical flower-head, of deep-purple colour in this case, and of a square regular shape. This variety is a native of the Mediterranean, and loves warmth but not excessive heat. It will flower best in the spring.

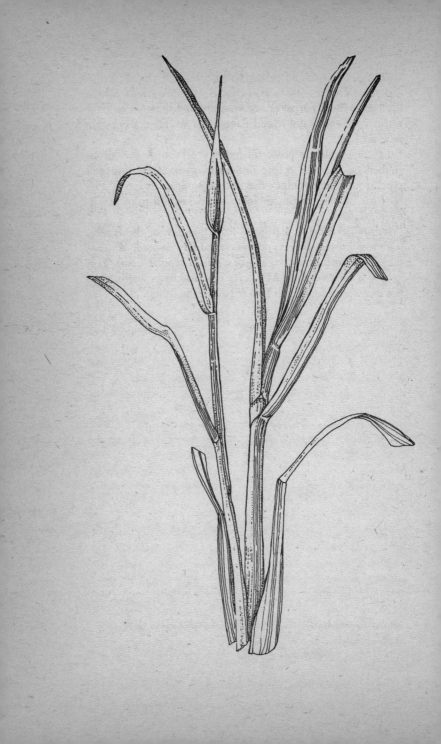

Lemongrass

Cymbopogon citratus JUNCACEAE

The "sweet rush", lemongrass, is an unusual herb, bearing great resemblance to the flax plant family in its appearance and habit of growth. The leaves are long straps of fresh bright green, sheathing the stems which grow from a fleshy base.

Lemongrass is a fast-growing herb, fitting happily into a courtyard planting, especially if a fountain or pool is near by. Its fleshy roots are always thirsty, but if given plenty of water it will thrive in the hottest position.

Not a very well-known herb, it should be used much more by those who wish to have a clear skin and bright eyes. It has very large amounts of natural vitamin A, and its aromatic oil is used in many skin-care preparations. Its usual method of use is in a tea, one or two fresh leaves chopped up very finely (or sliced with kitchen scissors), and boiling water poured on in the usual way. Let it stand for several minutes, add a little honey and a drop of lemon juice. It is an ideal nightcap.

The plant is quite handsome, and in one growing season should make a clump about 6 inches across at the base and 2 feet high. It can be increased by lifting the clump and pulling away rooted pieces from its outside edges, or a sharp spade can be used to break the offsets away from the main clump if you do not wish to up-end it altogether.

In my own propagating gardens, one small single stem of lemongrass was planted late one October. In mid-March the following season I lifted the clump to divide for nursery potting, and 49 new plants were the result. Admittedly, a very wet summer helped its growth along, but this will give you some idea of the space to allow for it in your garden layout, if your soil is rich and fertile and water can be had in abundance.

Lovage

Levisticum officinale UMBELLIFERAE

Lovage is a very difficult herb to grow in its germination and seedling stage, and also a very slow starter, and this seems to have discouraged many herb fanciers from cultivating it in their gardens.

The seeds take weeks and sometimes months to germinate and, unlike other herbs, need cool conditions for the best results. My first sowing of lovage taught me a lesson in patience. After some three or four weeks of warm weather, no sign of life could be seen in the seed box, and I put it aside in the potting room, meaning to remove the soil and try again with fresher seed. This was at the busiest seed-sowing time of year, in early spring, and another seed box got put on top of the lovage, and was watered and tended to provide me with new plants of sage. Cooler weather returned, and when I removed the sage box to pot out the seedlings some 8 weeks later I found about 25 little lovage plants in the box below, with their dicotyledon twin seed stems growing sturdily in the cool darkness.

Lovage seeds can be soaked in cool water for 24 hours before sowing, although I have not found this to speed up their germination by a very appreciable amount. I now sow lovage in the autumn, when cool nights help it along, and for old time's sake I put another seed box on top.

The plant is a tall, slow-growing perennial, taking four or more years to attain its full height. One plant of lovage in the garden is sufficient for a good-sized family, for it is a rampant grower when mature, with plenty of its shiny brilliant-green leaves available when needed. This is not a herb for those who like quick returns; but it is a stately, showy plant, well worth

137

the patience and time needed to bring it to maturity. It can be cut back hard from time to time to keep it shapely.

The leaves have a celery flavour, with a yeasty taste when added to soups and stews, and it is sometimes cooked in vegetarian dishes to give a "meaty" flavour for those who miss this in their diet. The Maggi brand seasonings have lovage as their chief ingredient.

Lovage is a close relative of the ginseng family, and has a long history of use in Asian cultures. In India it is used extensively as an antiseptic in times of cholera outbreaks, the blanched stems being chewed raw. In cold climates the tops may die down during the worst winter months, but in warmer areas it should continue green and useful all the year.

It needs careful watching in the early seedling stage: caterpillars, slugs and snails, and aphis too, love the new leaves as they uncurl. Use one of the "safe" sprays (see p. 36) to keep them away. Give the young plant a rich, deep soil with plenty of compost and blood and bone well under where the young roots are to lie, and then give moisture continuously; they need this to keep their slow spreading roots growing strongly. Good drainage is particularly necessary for this herb.

A tea made from lovage leaves and stems is very helpful in rheumatic conditions, to free the body of waste materials and stimulate the kidneys. A small handful of the herb to a half-pint of boiling water makes a pleasant drink, needing a pinch of salt rather than a teaspoon of honey, since it has the taste of a broth or stock.

See if a lovage bath will do for you what it did for the village maidens of the Middle Ages. The herb was freely used for its deodorizing properties, a handful or two of leaves being added (bruised, of course) to hot bath water. It was also worn in a cloth bag around the neck when going on a medieval "date" with the boyfriend, not as a superstitious love-charm or in order to weave a magic spell, but in the very prosaic role of a body-deodorant.

Compost in the soil is a must for lovage. Its roots spread and forage deeply, and its slow growth means that initial feeding and working of the ground is necessary to provide its needs for at least four years or more. So take time and care in preparation to get better results.

Persevere with those difficult seeds. The fresher they are the better they will germinate. The end result will be a magnificent plant for the back row in your herb garden. Use its leaves in many savoury dishes, in soups and stews, and fresh in salads.

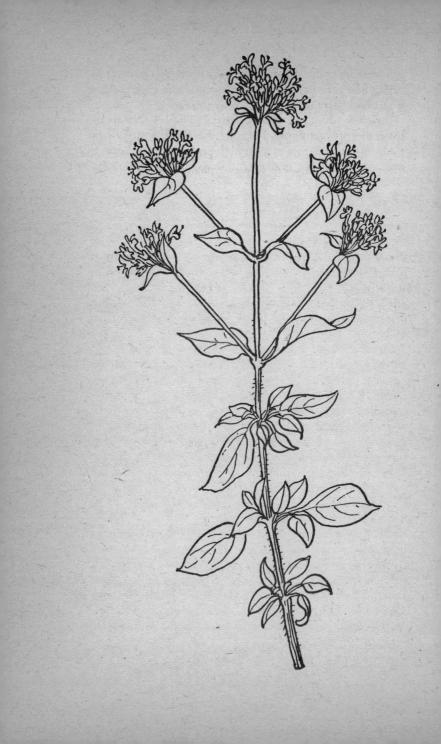

Marjoram

Origanum majorana LABIATAE

Oregano

Origanum vulgare LABIATAE

If you suffer from "dizzy spells" or the vapours, marjoram is the herb for you. What smelling salts will do, so will marjoram, and it is one herb whose flavour and aroma *increases* when dried. Keep some dried leaves handy in a sealed glass jar, and if someone faints on your carpet, bring out the "Joy of the Mountains".

Marjoram and oregano are very powerful antiseptic herbs when used both inside and outside, and taken freely in the diet can help maintain a high resistance to disease. No herb lover should ever be without one or other of them. Marjoram forms a small compact bush about 12 inches high, with light-green heart-shaped leaves and tiny white starry flowers growing in tight little bundles up the stem, which give it the name "knot marjoram" As with most herbs, a lot of strength and flavour leaves the plant when it flowers, so if you want it for culinary purposes, keep the flowering at bay by cutting and drying just when the buds start to form. Hang it in small bunches of 6 or 8 stems head downwards to dry, then rub the buds and leaves off the hard woody stems and store in sealed glass jars. Even the dead stems retain much perfume, so chop these, store them separately and add to your next barbecue fire when the first fierce heat has died down. They will give the meat a slight flavour which your guests will be curious to identify. Keep the secret if you like, and keep them guessing through the meal.

Grow marjoram in a sunny spot in light soil, with a good

deal of water during the heat of the summer. It will withstand dryness, but like most herbs grows even more contentedly with water to keep its rather soft leaves in good condition. It is evergreen, and a hardy perennial, but its flavour may deteriorate after several years, so it is best to strike cuttings or layer it to ensure a continuing supply of young plants with which to replace the older ones every 3 or 4 years. My own favourite marjoram plant is now 4 years old, and showing no signs of senility; but to be on the safe side I have several young plants waiting in the wings in other parts of the garden. Cuttings will root readily if taken in early spring before any flowering stems are formed, or in early autumn when the stalks are strong and more woody, and less likely to wilt. Take slips with some old wood attached.

Oregano, or wild marjoram, is the parent stock from which the garden marjoram was developed. Its flavour is stronger, but its appearance and growth is otherwise very similar. It layers itself more easily than garden marjoram, and its flowers are at the end of longer stems in a tight, square-shaped formation. In this country, oregano does not have the biting pungency of flavour it has in its home territory, the Mediterranean. It also grows wild and aromatic in Mexico and parts of South America, having been taken to America by the Pilgrim Fathers and naturalized there, but soil conditions do change the flavour slightly, and in Australia it becomes almost indistinguishable from marjoram. If you happen to live in one of the few areas of basalt or rich volcanic soil, you will have ideal conditions to grow oregano at its spicy best.

Both marjoram and oregano have, like basil, a natural affinity for tomato dishes, and for the farinaceous specialities of Italian cuisine, the pastas, pizza and lasagne dishes. Add a sprig to the hot oil when making the tomato-based sauce for these. Oregano is added to the thick vegetable soups and casserole dishes of Mexico, too.

Here is an eighteenth-century French recipe that will taste just as delectable with the stronger oregano or the milder marjoram:

142

Marinaded Veal Chops

Slice a pocket in veal chops, and insert an anchovy fillet in each one. Make a marinade of equal parts of oil and vinegar, to which a crushed garlic clove and crushed fresh oregano has been added. Steep the meat in this marinade for at least 2 hours, turning once. Remove, and blot dry. Then brown the chops in oil or butter and transfer them to a casserole. Add ½ cup of dry white wine, a few drops of lemon juice, shallots and parsley, and cover tightly. Bake in a moderate oven for 30 minutes, or till tender. Cream can be substituted for the wine for a variation.

If you are a cole-slaw addict as I am, try this "hot-slaw" in the winter time for a change.

Hot Herb Slaw

Shred half a cabbage. Melt two tablespoons of butter in a large heavy pan, and fry the cabbage for several minutes, stirring to prevent its sticking, then add a half-cup of water, sprigs of basil, dill and oregano to taste. Mix through, simmer several minutes then stir in ¾ cup of yoghurt. Heat again quickly and serve.

Does your hair come out in handfuls on the brush or comb? Make a strong infusion of marjoram: 2 handfuls of the fresh herb in a cup of water, and simmer gently for a few minutes, then let stand till lukewarm. Rub this solution well into the scalp after washing and rinsing the hair, and gently pat dry. It conditions and strengthens the hair as well.

Marjoram oil can be rubbed into joints and sinews if they start to stiffen or cramp after heavy exercise, particularly in the cold weather. You can make your own quite easily (see p. 26). And if you get a toothache right in the middle of Christmas dinner, chew leaves of marjoram over the spot to deaden the ache until you can rouse out your dentist. Marjoram used regularly in the diet helps to ward off stomach upsets and acts through the bloodstream as an internal antiseptic against those tummy "wogs".

Altogether, a happy and rejoiceful herb.

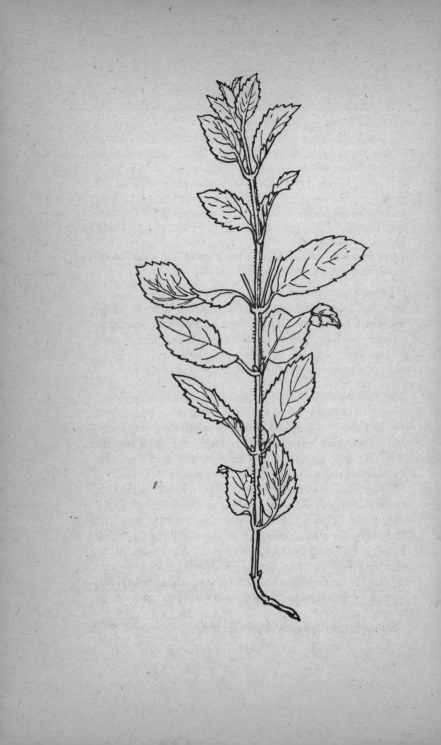

Mint

Various types LABIATAE

All the Mint family need water and more water, but never, never let their roots lie in soggy, badly drained ground. Mint will grow almost anywhere provided these two necessities are available—water and good drainage.

In warm climates mint will grow in partial shade or full sun (although too much shade will cause it to grow tall and spindly), and indeed will grow so vigorously that it is advisable to confine it in some way: in a walled bed, raised above the ground; in a large terra-cotta pot (12 or 14 inches will do); or, if you want it in the open garden, try sinking an 18-inch length of terra-cotta drainpipe upright in the garden, and plant your mint in this. If on the other hand, you have a large garden, and do not mind odd stalks of mint among the hydrangeas and gladioli, by all means plant your mint and let it wander. I grow all my mints both ways, my stock plants confined to large tubs and odd plants here and there in my garden. When I am weeding, the sudden sweet fragrance of applemint or sharp spearmint tells me my mints are on the move again.

All the mint varieties will inter-pollinate, and sorting out the species can be a headache. Try to grow them away from each other if you are a purist, for their flavours will eventually become adulterated if cross-pollination occurs. Alternatively, nip off all flowering stems as they appear—sometimes a tedious job, but well worth it to preserve the flavour.

Some of the many types are listed here:

APPLEMINT. Soft, woolly, downy leaves, with a rounded shape, and a strong apple taste and perfume.

VARIEGATED APPLEMINT. Creamy yellow and light-green

patched leaf, a very handsome plant. Not quite as much flavour as above. Will grow in open sunlight better than most.

EAU-DE-COLOGNE MINT. A most exotic perfume when crushed, as its name implies. This is a favourite for a perfumed bath. Dry the mint leaves and store in an airtight jar, or use a handful of the fresh leaves, well-bruised, in hot bath water.

SPEARMINT (*Mentha spicata*). Smoother sharp-pointed leaves, the best all-purpose flavouring mint. Used by the Romans and taken by them to Britain. Grown in monastery gardens. This variety can be affected badly by a type of rust disease which starts in the roots. The stems and leaves will discolour and the roots when lifted will be pulpy and rotten. Lift the whole mint patch and burn it, dig lime or dolomite well into the soil, and leave it for a season. Do not plant mint there again. A good soil, well fed and well limed in the first place, has less chance of incubating this destructive disease.

Spearmint planted near roses and other plants will deter aphis.

PEPPERMINT (*Mentha piperita*). This mint was known to the early Chaldeans as a soothing and pleasant digestive aid. The Romans also used it this way, and the custom persists in our "after-dinner mint". It was cultivated by the ancient Egyptians, and by the middle of the eighteenth century was in general use in Britain. A pleasant drink for flatulence can be made by chopping a few leaves into a cup, half filling it with boiling water, covering and leaving for five minutes. Sip slowly.

Peppermint oil is a handy home remedy. It stimulates the cold-perceiving nerves, and thus is good for rheumatic and muscular aches and pains, particularly in winter, giving a sensation of warmth in the affected area.

Peppermint is a low-growing, creeping plant with small purplish leaves and long runners rooting into the soil. It needs more water than the others, especially if grown in full sun, where its flavour and oil content will be higher.

Stinging nettle (*Urtica dioica*) planted near peppermint will double the amount of essential oil from the plant. Commercial growers may care to take advantage of Nature's help once again, to increase their yield without cost or danger to themselves, the soil, or posterity.

Do not confuse peppermint oil with the peppermint essence used as a flavouring. The essence has an alcohol base. The strength and penetrating power of peppermint oil can be of great relief to sufferers from a heavy head cold. A few drops on the corner of your handkerchief can be inhaled, freeing the head of that stuffed-up misery, and if you are at home you can add a few drops to a bowl of boiling water, put a towel over your head, and inhale the pleasant fumes. If you are in bed, a tissue with a few drops on it can be placed near the bedhead, and it will effectively clear your breathing passages all night. (Make sure not to get the oil anywhere near your eyes.)

GARDEN MINT. The common roundish-leaved type, with a more mellow flavour, and a strong sturdy habit of growth. It does best in full sunshine, and will grow well in a pot on the patio or near the kitchen door.

To increase your mint plants, chop downwards into the bed with a sharp spade or hoe in the early spring, and a new rooted plant will spring from each piece. It can be then dug up and potted or given away. Root division is easy too, many new plants being gained from one length of root which has been chopped off at each junction. Give all the mints soil rich in organic matter and humus, and lime or dolomite is essential.

Now for some recipes that benefit from mint's cool flavour.

Country Fruit Bake

Soak 4 oz. dried apples and 4 oz. dried apricots (separately) in hot water just come off the boil, for ¾ hour, then drain. (You can drink the liquid later when it has cooled.) Butter a shallow oven-proof dish. Cut a banana into inch-long sections and arrange over the bottom, then add the drained fruit and 5 or 6 leaves of garden mint or spearmint, and pour over the top half a cup of sweet cider in which 3 tablespoons of honey have been dissolved. Sprinkle generously with fine-grated lemon-rind, dot with butter and bake uncovered at 300 degrees for 1½ to 2 hours, or till fruit is tender and glazed.

Mint Chutney
2 lb. apples
4 oz. raisins
1 teaspoon dry mustard
¼ cup chopped mint
¾ pint vinegar
4 oz. brown sugar
2 teaspoons salt
½ teaspoon pepper

Peel and core the apples, and mince or chop finely with the raisins. Add all the other ingredients and cook all together until of jam-like consistency. Bottle immediately, and seal well.

Mint and Raisin Sandwich Filling
Mix equal quantities of chopped raisins and mint leaves with a little hot water to give a spreadable consistency.

For a Cold Platter
Whip cream cheese through with a little top-of-the-milk, add a few caraway, dill or fennel seeds. Form into little balls and serve with chunks of fresh pineapple topped with an applemint or pineapple mint leaf.

Lemon Cucumber
Peel and slice thinly a firm fresh cucumber. Arrange in layers with salt, lemon juice and chopped fresh garden mint leaves in between. Garnish with a dob of sour cream.

Beetroot and Mint Salad
1 lb. cooked beetroot
2 tablespoons chopped mint
French dressing
Lettuce

Peel and slice the beetroot. Wash and dry lettuce and arrange on a large platter. Pour over the french dressing and garnish with the chopped mint.

Mint Jelly

1 pint water
1 lb cooking apples
1½ cups of mint
Green colouring
Sugar
Juice of 1 lemon

Wash the apples, chop coarsely (no need to peel or core), and simmer in the water until the fruit is pulp. Strain the mixture by hanging in a muslin or jelly bag overnight. For each pint of juice, add 1 lb of sugar and boil rapidly until thick. Allow to cool, then stir in the lemon juice, finely-shredded mint and a few drops of green colouring. Seal in small glass jars.

Parsley

Petroselinum crispum UMBELLIFERAE
Petroselinum sativum

Parsley well deserves its place as the most widely used of all herbs. And it is true that there is often more goodness and nutrition in those sprigs of garnish left on the plate than there is in the dish itself. So eat up every little bit, and bless Mother Nature for her bounty.

Parsley contains vitamins A, B and C in the leaves and larger quantities of C in the roots, approximately three times as much as oranges. Its vitamin A content is more than that found in cod liver oil. It contains the fatty acids necessary to utilize in the body the fat-soluble vitamins, and is rich in minerals of which iron is the most important, but calcium, sodium and magnesium are also present. Apiol, the oily non-volatile liquid found in root and leaves is a powerful digestive aid in the quantities found in the parsley plant, and another substance, apiin, a form of pectin, also helps in this process. Parsley stimulates the whole digestive system, and also the kidneys, to promote healthy action in this most important organ. If your kidneys are unhappy, then so are you; so keep them healthy and functioning well with the addition of parsley every day in your diet.

The herb is as valuable to most animals as it is to humans, although *never* give it to birds of any type or to pet rabbits. It does not suit their digestive processes at all, and has even been fatal to cage birds.

Pliny, that wise old Roman, was one of the first to extol the virtues of parsley. He sprinkled it on his fish-ponds, observing the increase in the health and vitality as well as the number of the inhabitants. So as far back as the first century A.D., parsley

151

gained a reputation it has never lost, that of increasing virility in males and fertility in females. The giving by one woman to another of a parsley root still today brings forth the remark, "Well, you should be pregnant within the year." I like to think it is due not to an "old wives' tale" but to the increased vitality and enjoyment of life that a parsley plant in the garden will give you if you eat some every day.

Parsley is a highly valued addition to a dog's diet, and natural rearing methods for dogs make great use of it. As a general tonic, to keep liver and kidneys functioning well, parsley should be sprinkled over the dog's meal every few days. My own little long-haired Corgi is a walking advertisement for parsley and kelp. Born with her head on one side, and unable to be bred or shown, she was to be destroyed until we took her as a household pet. Now three years old, she has the constitution and endurance (and appetite!) of a Great Dane, and she was reared on fresh meat with parsley and kelp as dietary supplements, and horseradish leaves and garlic to keep her worm-free and healthy.

To the ancient Greeks, "to be in need of parsley" was to be gravely ill. To them, only parsley was powerful enough to be of use *in extremis.*

Parsley can be very slow to germinate, and no doubt much of its reputation of being hard to grow stems from this. It can take anywhere from five days to eight weeks, and must be kept moist all the time. An old English phrase says it goes nine times to the Devil and back before it germinates; and he likes it so much he keeps some of it. I have always found it much easier than its reputation suggests, if a good potting mixture is used in the seed box. This gives the shoot no hard crust of soil or sand to force its way through, and my parsley seedlings have never taken longer than 14 days. Soaking the seed in warm water first is also recommended before planting, but I have found a simple way to get the same effect. Sow your parsley seed on soil that has been soaked with water, cover with about ⅛ inch of seed-box mixture, then place the box out in the hottest sunny spot with a sheet of clear polythene plastic over the top in which a few air holes have been cut. Leave the box out all day, and your parsley seed should by nightfall have got the message. Next day and afterwards, just give it the usual seed-box care.

Ample nitrogen is needed for parsley to produce abundant leaves, so keep the compost content of your soil very high, with any animal manures you can lay your hands on, too. It will grow well in a trough or pot, and unit-dwellers will find it a herb they can have success with: a sunny or partially shaded balcony suits it very well.

The leaves dry easily in a luke-warm oven. Rub them through your hands to crumble them when dry, and store for convenience near your food preparation area in the kitchen, to remind you to use parsley with a liberal hand.

So many recipes abound where parsley is used that here I will give you only a tasty seventeenth-century one.

Green Chicken
Take 6 chicken breasts, bones removed where possible, and skin them. Divide into flat portions. Dredge with seasoned flour and shake off the excess. Dip into egg and milk, coat thoroughly with fine breadcrumbs. Sauté over medium heat till cooked through. Remove, and let cool enough to handle. Coat the top side of each piece with beaten egg, then press on the chopped parsley, making sure it adheres to the chicken. Bake in a warm oven for about 10 minutes.

Italian or Hamburg Parsley (*P. sativum*) is a taller, flat-leaved type mainly grown for its root, the flavour of which is a blend of parsley and parsnip. The root can be dug at the end of the first growing season, and sliced thinly to add to soups or Irish stews, casseroles and many other savoury dishes. Thin slices of the root can also be sautéed in butter and served alone as a vegetable. I think the green leaves of this variety have even more flavour than the curly common type, and they grow so large that you will always have enough and to spare.

So, Ogden Nash, parsley is *not* garsley!

153

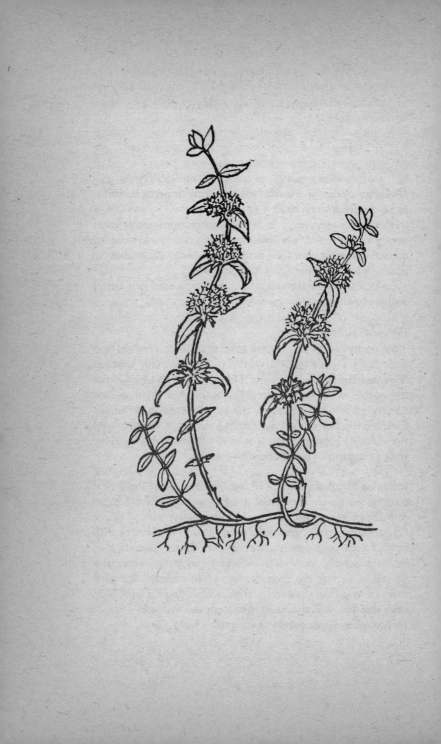

Pennyroyal

Mentha pulegium LABIATAE

"Pudding Grasse" is one country name for pennyroyal, which in Scotland was used to flavour the traditional haggis. "Lurk-in-the-ditch" is another, as indeed it does, growing in low, boggy ground with no apparent ill-effects. It is a creeping ground-cover, a very useful plant for carpeting a difficult shady corner with its minty bright green leaves. It flowers through the summer, with 6-inch stems of fluffy mauve whorls at each leaf junction. It will also grow quite well in full sun, provided it has ample water and perhaps some shelter given by surrounding plants.

Pennyroyal is easy to grow, free from insect pests, and very useful to plant anywhere you have ant-nests you want to eradicate. Crazy paving and flagstones often suffer from sandy little ant-mounds at a cracked joint; so plant pennyroyal here and there in pockets, and you will be ant-free in no time.

Not a generation ago, an ointment made from pennyroyal was used as a mosquito and flea repellent, and you can get the same effect when gardening or bushwalking by rubbing some fresh leaves briskly over exposed skin. It will also deter ants from raiding your kitchen shelves if you sprinkle crushed pennyroyal leaves about. The perfume is delightful to us, but ants will be off and away as quickly as they can.

In the days of the sailing-ships, dried pennyroyal leaves were added to the water casks to keep them fresh and wholesome.

Dry some of the beautiful flowering stems in spring and summer, and cut them into sections with a circlet of mauve blossom on each one. Add them to pot-pourri mixtures for a less sweet but cooler fragrance than usual, and make sure you put this mix in transparent containers to enjoy the colour.

A tea made from the leaves is good for depression. The usual quantity of a small handful to a cup of boiling water is plenty. Add honey or a slice of orange to this one: it is delicious.

For a change instead of using mint or parsley, garnish parboiled or steamed tiny new potatoes with pennyroyal leaves. Add a nob of butter to the saucepan when they are cooked, then the herb leaves, and shake gently about to spread the taste. Use only a few leaves. They are quite strong in flavour.

The herb's power as an insecticide, especially against fleas, is denoted in its name, Mentha pulegium or "Flea Mint", so your dog could also benefit from having its coat rubbed with the crushed leaves and stems of pennyroyal, and a few leaves sprinkled on its blanket every few days should ensure flea-free bedding too.

Pennyroyal has been prescribed for everything from "the itch" to jaundice, and the old herbal writers placed great store by it wherever warming, soothing and cleansing of the body was required. It was placed under the dominion of Venus, and was also prescribed almost automatically for any female complaints.

Haggis

Try this simplified haggis recipe if the traditional time-consuming one is inconvenient for you. (By the time those brawny lads and fetching lassies have come to the haggis-stage of the festivities, they will probably not notice any difference anyway!)

8 oz. sheep's liver
4 oz. beef suet
2 onions
1 heaped cup oatmeal
Salt and black pepper
A few chopped pennyroyal sprigs

Boil the liver in water to cover for ¾ hour. Drain, and keep the liquid. Chop up the liver very finely. Steam the onions till tender and chop up very small with the suet. Brown the oatmeal very quickly in an oiled heavy pan over medium heat. Combine all the ingredients, add the salt and pepper and chopped pennyroyal and moisten with the saved liquid. Turn into a greased pudding bowl, cover with a cloth and steam for two hours. Decorate the upturned pudding with more sprigs of pennyroyal to serve.

Rosemary

Rosmarinus officinalis LABIATAE

In America, in 1550, an unknown author who wrote "A Lytel Herball" said, "Take the flowers of Rosemary and put them in a lynen clothe, and so boyle them in fayre cleane water to the halfe and cole it and drynke it for it is much worth against all the evyls in the body." He (or she) was confirming the age-old power of rosemary as a beneficial herb for all parts of the body.

The gipsies revere this herb above all others for its beneficial effect on skin and hair. Pure rosemary oil (obtained commercially by distillation) is the best conditioner in the world for tresses either fair, dark or burnished copper, and keeps the scalp in good condition too. Many shampoos now contain it, but the pure oil gives a wonderful result. Rub a few drops well into the scalp (it will not make the hair greasy), and repeat regularly after each washing and drying of the hair. Silky, soft and healthy hair will be the result. You can also make a tonic rinse from fresh rosemary. Take a small handful of the sprays, chop or bruise well in a mortar, then add a large cup of boiling water. Let stand for an hour or longer if you wish. Use after the normal rinsing, and do not dry off too hard with the towel. The more rosemary is left the sweeter your hair will smell. Rosemary water will tone up your skin, too. You can even drink it to deodorize and sweeten your breath. It is the chief ingredient in true eau-de-Cologne.

Homemade rosemary oil (see p. 26) can be used like thyme oil to dispel a headache caused by overstrain or prolonged concentration, and prevent unwanted crows'-feet forming around the eyes. Just rub a few drops into the temples, and feel the tension relax in minutes.

Dried rosemary and coltsfoot have been used together with sage to make a smoking mixture that will not irritate a sufferer from asthma who refuses to give up his beloved "chimney". This mixture is not only quite harmless, but is indeed beneficial to health, for these herbs are used to combat chest, lung and throat complaints medicinally. A quick whizz through the kitchen blender will shred the herb "tobacco" nicely for you.

On the food front, rosemary oil can be rubbed over a joint before baking. Cut a few slits here and there in the meat and rub the oil well into them. I have already mentioned its wonderful way with the lowly sausage (see p. 26). Add a rosemary sprig to all boiled meats, corned beef, lamb and pork. Ham, either baked or boiled, must have rosemary to give it that pine flavour and perfume. Be a bit sparing with the fresh herb until you find your family's tastes. One lady complained sadly to me that her husband and children would not eat the lamb she had roasted with rosemary. She had cut many little slits in the skin and put a large sprig of rosemary in each one —baked rosemary flavoured with lamb! Just add a little at first. Too much can be overpowering.

Rosemary and remembrance are often mentioned in the same breath. The origins of its association with memory and constancy, friendship and trust, go back to man's very earliest records in the western parts of Asia where it was grown on the graves of ancestors to invoke their help and guidance for the living. Sprigs are still traditionally carried at weddings, and also at funerals, and on many occasions where solemn vows and pledges are made. Rosemary tea was taken to improve and strengthen the brain and failing memory.

A native of the warm, sunny sea coasts of Spain, Portugal, France and Italy, where its perfume can often be smelt far out to sea, rosemary is known and cultivated all over the world. It grows best near salt water, and is a valuable garden shrub for seaside dwellers. Sandy light loam suits it best, and it is hardy and drought-resistant, too. Too much water will cause some of the leaves to drop, but normally it will grow under difficult or exposed conditions very well. The more sunshine the better, to build up its stores of oil in the leaves and flowers.

In late winter, when other herbs are well and truly asleep in the cold ground, rosemary starts to flower. It is a valuable plant for bees at this time, when other nectar is scarce, and will bear its white or pale blue flowers right into spring. The prostrate variety (*Rosmarinus prostratus*), is valuable for rockeries and sunny hot corners, and its spreading growth is most attractive beside brick or stone steps. Reflected heat from walls is a tonic for the plant and it will give its perfume more freely under these conditions.

Slow-growing at first, rosemary can live to a great age, over thirty years or more. To grow from cuttings, take a small side stem with a heel of old wood attached, and strike this time in a more sandy soil mixture. It will grow well in a pot, and can be trimmed to a formal shape if required.

A recipe for dressed-up spaghetti comes from southern France, where rosemary grows on the hillsides.

Spaghetti in Herb Sauce

3 tablespoons olive oil
1 cup chopped onions
2 tablespoons chopped parsley
1 clove garlic (crushed)
1 stalk celery (chopped fine)
Rosemary leaves to taste
2 firm tomatoes
½ cup white wine
Grated Parmesan cheese
1 lb. spaghetti, cooked and drained
Salt and pepper

Heat the oil in a large heavy saucepan. Sauté the onions till lightly brown, then add the herbs and cook over a low heat for 5 minutes. Add the tomatoes, and cook lightly. Mix in the wine, salt and pepper, and heat through for a minute. Pour over the hot spaghetti, and sprinkle the cheese on top.

Rue

Ruta graveolens RUTACEAE

Rue is a herb that today means to many of us only a plant carried by Hamlet's Ophelia, and therefore signifying sorrow and dire misfortune. Early herb writers revelled in the knowledge we have now lost of its amazingly strong powers, in particular those affecting eyesight and counteracting poisons. Present-day crime has veered away from poison as a means of settling a score or removing a political enemy; but in the Greek and Roman Empires, a knowledge of antidotes often meant life itself. Rue had an almost magical reputation for warding off or counteracting evil, and even long before this it was known to the Druids and the ancient Saxons as a holy herb and strewn in homes and public places. Later, Christian churches used it too, the twigs for sprinkling Holy Water being taken from the bush. Dioscorides noted that a weasel, when going out snake-hunting for food, often ate rue first, and from this observation came later experiments using it as a poison antidote. It was the principal ingredient in mithridate, the legendary antidote for all poisons ever concocted, and was the plant given by Mercury to Ulysses to overcome the poisons (both physical and mental) of Circe. Dioscorides also noted another peculiarity of rue: it can raise a nasty inflammation when handled by some people with sensitive skins. So if you wish to grow it, treat it with suitable care.

Rue was much in demand amongst the artisans, craftsmen, sculptors and painters of the Renaissance period as a strengthener of eyesight. A weak tea was brewed from the leaves and taken inwardly, and the eyes were bathed each day with a similar solution. The herb is a very powerful one, so be careful if you wish to follow in the steps of Leonardo and Michelangelo, who both used it, claiming it gave them not only strengthened and improved vision but inner sight and creativity as well.

Like most so-called superstitions, the belief in rue's great powers has a sound basis of practical common sense. Rutin, its most active ingredient, was found during the last World War to be of great value in the treatment of weakened blood-vessels, and it is this property that makes it so effective an eye-strengthener, by increasing the capillary action and blood supply to the vision centre. Some have pointed to the Doctrine of Signatures again, for the strange root formation of rue bears quite a resemblance to the arrangement of the blood vessels in the eye.

Rue is certainly not a culinary herb. It has a strong fetid odour, which gives it another important use—as an insect repellent in the garden. No sane insect or animal (other than the before-mentioned weasel) will come within sniffing distance of rue. Up to the end of last century, judges and court dignitaries in England carried small bunches of rue, and it was also strewn freely around the courtroom, to act as an insect and pest repellent. The dreaded "jail fever" was carried by fleas and cockroaches, and rue was originally used in this way to prevent its spread into the courtroom by way of the prisoners.

The plant, as if to make up for its unpleasant odour, is an extremely attractive little herb of about 2 feet in height, with lacy bluish foliage and yellow flowers in summer. It is a perennial and evergreen, too. An insect repellent powder can be made from the leaves. Dry them and crush finely, then sprinkle them around and on any insect-infested plant. Within an hour the pests will be scampering, crawling or flying away as fast as possible.

The seeds germinate slowly, and when finally through the soil they appear to be crawling about all over the seed box with downy little feelers. Sow them in the spring, and transplant when the seedlings are big enough to handle. You should not need gloves at this early stage of their growth.

A border of rue can be very effective, as its greyish-blue foliage makes delicate counterpoint with the true greens more

164

common in the flower garden. For a striking ribbon of colour around formal beds, plant rue all along the edge, santolina (a grey feathery-soft plant with brilliant yellow flower-cushions in spring) inside it, then balance these two with another planting of blue rosemary behind. As a border for a large rose-garden, this tri-coloured hedge can be quite spectacular.

Sage

Salvia officinalis LABIATAE

Here is another herb of Jupiter, bringing long life, with an active old age and all faculties in good working order. Sage is well named, coming from the Latin *salvere*, to save, and cultures much older (and perhaps wiser) than ours used it as a daily beverage, just as we drink tea.

The Chinese drank sage tea as often as possible, and their early records show how high a value was placed on its health-giving properties. Indeed, 4 lb. of China tea was exchanged by Chinese merchants with Britain for every pound of sage tea grown in England. Both countries were well-pleased with the deal. I wonder which one really had the best of the bargain?

The herb is low-growing, to about 1 foot in height, and is a compact, rather bushy plant. Its greyish-green leaves, with the rough texture of a cat's tongue, make good teeth-cleaners, and at Tunbridge Wells they are given to spa clients to clean their teeth after taking the discolouring mineral waters. The flowers are deep purple bells, produced in spring, but if you want the herb for the table, nip off the flowering stems when they appear. The seeds are rather large for a small plant, round black balls which can be slow to germinate. Keep the seed box rather drier than usual. This will often start the seedlings on their way. You can soak the seed in warm water if you wish, to soften the hard outer shell before planting.

Sage needs an alkaline soil, so use plenty of dolomite and scatter a handful through the topsoil when preparing a place for the plants. Hot sun and dryness will give you a sturdy bush in a very short time, but watch for any sign of "wet feet" in prolonged wet weather, and move your plant to a drier location. Sage can be a bit pernickety and will sometimes

167

shrivel and die almost overnight for no apparent reason if the weather or soil conditions are not to its liking. Caterpillars are very fond of it, and must be picked off before they can strip the leaves. Dried sage leaves do not keep their flavour as well as most dry herbs, so pick them fresh if you can for culinary use.

A delightful tobacco substitute can be made from dried sage leaves, the slight lessening of the fresh flavour being an advantage, since sage can be rather overpowering in its strength. Sage cigarettes would not be so revolutionary: the herb was inhaled in snuff when this habit was fashionable.

Sage tea has a long history of therapeutic use: for rheumatic complaints, and more especially to strengthen the brain and heart and quicken the memory and senses. Sage leaves on bread and butter are still eaten regularly in northern England and Scotland, and the Chinese credit their longevity to liberal use of the herb. Rub the leaves on gums under dentures, too, to stimulate and harden them. The tea is made by adding 1 cup of boiling water to a dessertspoon of fresh (or a teaspoon of dried) sage leaves. Cover and leave 5 minutes. Sip slowly. It also calms excitement, so make a pot straight away if you win the lottery.

To Darken Grey Hair

For centuries the gipsies have used sage to darken grey hair, and here are several recipes, both modern and ancient (one comes from the Rome of Tiberius) for you to try.

1. Add 1 teaspoon of dried sage (1 tablespoon of fresh) and an equal quantity of China tea to half a pint of water in a jar. Stand the jar in a pot of boiling water for two hours, then strain and squeeze well. Rub in a little of the liquid each second day on damp hair.

2. Add a good handful of fresh sage leaves to half a pint of water just off the boil. Then add a teaspoonful of borax and allow to get cold. Dip your hairbrush in this liquid and gently brush through your locks. Repeat as often as necessary.

3. Add a good handful of fresh sage leaves, well bruised, to one pint of boiling water. Steep for about 30 minutes for a

lighter colour, several hours for a darker one. Strain, and cool. Pour the sage rinse over the hair, working it well through with the fingertips or with a brush. Catch the run-off in a basin, and repeat the process several times. Gently dry off.

In the kitchen, sage is synonymous with stuffing. Most mixtures for seasoning poultry and game make use of it, not only for its aromatic flavour, but for its now lesser-known virtue of breaking down the fats and oils in the meat, thus aiding its digestion. Use it, too, with vegetables, and with cheese.

Stuffed Onions
Parboil 12 large onions (mild ones are best) for 8 minutes in salted water. Drain, scoop out the centres, leaving walls about ¼-inch thick, and fill with the following mixture: ½ cup chopped centres of the onions, ½ cup cooked and diced cold meat, 1 cup diced, cooked potatoes, chopped sage leaves, salt and pepper. Brush the onions with melted butter, arrange in a buttered baking-dish, sprinkle the breadcrumbs over, dot with butter, and bake in a moderate oven for about 35 minutes. If you want crisp outsides, brown the onions under the griller for the last 5 minutes. Brush them with more butter before you do.

If you are starting off a new garden and your soil is rocky and sandy, sage is one herb you can grow immediately, without preparation. It thrives on rather poor soil, and I suspect some of its bad reputation for suddenly giving up the ghost is caused by over- not under-feeding. It must have an alkaline soil, and perhaps this is also why it grows so well in a new garden where there is often a residue left in the topsoil of the builder's mortar and lime. Sage will grow well on a balcony for flat dwellers if it is given a concrete container. This provides the alkaline soil so necessary to help it flourish.

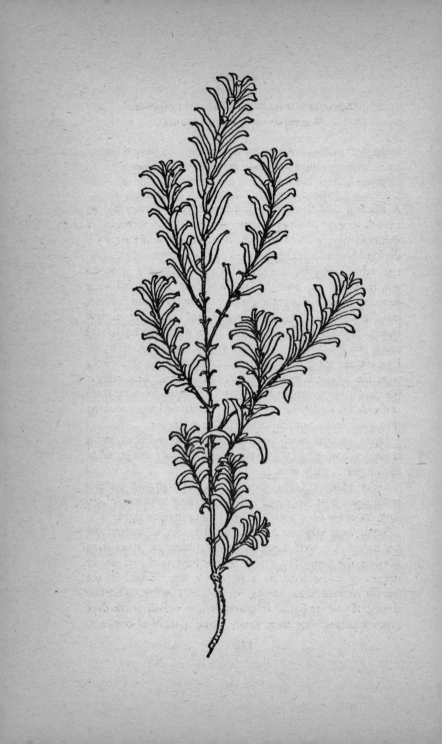

Savory

Summer savory *Satureia hortensis* LABIATAE
Winter savory *Satureia montana*

A beloved culinary herb of ancient Greece, savory has an annual variety, summer savory, as well as the perennial or winter savory. Both have similar flavour, and winter savory is the kind I have found best to grow. It is evergreen, of a spreading rather low habit of growth, with woody little stems on which appear tiny starry white flowers in spring and early summer. It has a pleasant aroma when the leaves are crushed, and a special affinity for beans, peas, and the squash and marrow family. A sprig added to the water when steaming chokos will make you wonder why they are still such a lowly vegetable. Remove the sprig after cooking, as the hard stem is not very palatable. The herb is used in sauces and to flavour herb vinegar (see p. 25) and the softer leaves can be stripped from the stem and added sparingly to soups, too. It will stand longer cooking than most herbs, with no deterioration in flavour.

Open sun suits savory well, and moderate conditions, and it is easily grown either from seed or hard-wood cuttings, taken in summer or early autumn.

Often added to herbal medicines for its warming qualities and pleasant taste, disguising some of the more unpalatable herb flavours, it has been used also, like rue, to sharpen sight.

Savory was taken to America by early British settlers, and has naturalized well. Crushed leaves rubbed on a bee-sting alleviate the pain. Try a few well-bruised sprigs of savory steeped in white wine for a refreshing tonic drink. If the flavour of basil is too strong for you in a recipe, substitute savory. If you are partial to young button squash or the dark green zucchini, slice them thinly, sauté quickly in butter to

171

which a savory sprig has been added, and serve immediately.

An unusual conserve can be made using the herb. It goes equally well with cold meat as a garnishing jelly or on toast as a jam. Try it drizzled over ice-cream too, as a piquant sauce. Top the dish with a sprig of fresh applemint or pineapple mint.

Savory and Grape Juice Jelly

1 can dark or light grape juice (small)
A good handful of savory, chopped
4 oz. powdered pectin
3 cups raw sugar
Juice of 1 lemon

Heat the grape juice and savory together, add the pectin, sugar and lemon and bring to the boil for 2 minutes, stirring all the time. Remove from the heat, strain out the savory, and seal in small jars immediately. You can put it, too, into decorative glasses, seal the top with polythene and an elastic band, and give it away as a gift to your friends.

Savory keeps its flavour well when dried. Strip the leaves from the stems, and store as usual.

Herbed Zucchini

1½ lbs zucchini
1 clove garlic, crushed
Small handful winter savory sprigs
4 large tomatoes
A little oil
1 large onion
Salt and black pepper
Mozzarella cheese
A little flour

Heat a little oil in a heavy pan and sauté the chopped onions and crushed garlic clove, the savory sprigs and the chopped onions for 10 minutes. Remove the savory sprigs. (These are quite woody and not chewable at all.) Purée in an electric blender or through a sieve, and set aside. Cut the uncooked

172

unpeeled zucchini crossways in thin slices, toss them lightly in the flour then brown quickly on both sides in a little more hot oil. Arrange them in an ovenproof serving dish, alternating layers of zucchini and sauce, ending with the sauce and thinly-sliced mozzarella cheese to cover the top. Sprinkle with paprika if desired. Cook in a moderate oven, uncovered, for 30 minutes.

French Sorrel

Rumex acetosa POLYGONACEAE

French sorrel is the best variety for the table. It is not so acid as the British native variety, and its sharp astringent taste will wake up a bland salad if a few small leaves are chopped and mixed through. Be a bit sparing with the vinegar or lemon juice in any dressing for such a salad, as sorrel has sufficient of its own oxalic acid.

It is a perennial pot-herb, similar to spinach (and it can be cooked like that vegetable), with bright, glossy-green spade-shaped leaves with a reddish touch to their stems. Growing in a small clump, it does not take up very much space and two or three plants should provide you with ample leaves for salads and soups. It is a relative of buckwheat, and of the dock family of "weeds", and is often mistakenly classed in with the other sorrels, of which oxalis is the most notorious member. Some of these other varieties can infiltrate pasturelands and become a real nuisance to the farmer, and they need no introduction to the home gardener, either. French Sorrel has no such propensity, keeping itself to itself in any sunny well-fed corner of the herb or vegetable garden.

Sorrel is easy to raise from seed in the spring, or from root divisions taken in the autumn. The seed keeps its germinating power well, and the young plants should break through the soil in about 7 to 10 days. They are sturdy-stemmed and easy to handle, and can be set out in the garden quite soon after the first two leaves are shooting. Guard them well from snails and slugs right from the first day, and give plenty of water to keep the leaves large and juicy. Cut off any flower heads that form, unless you need some fresh seed.

Juice from the leaves of sorrel can be used like rennet for

setting junket. Add drops to a cup of warm milk until it sours and sets, or make a strong "brew"—a handful of the herb in half a cup of water, and use this liquid when cool to set the junket in the same way. Juice from the leaves can also be used as a bleach for stains on linen, particularly for iron, rust or mould stains.

Sorrel is a strong internal antiseptic, and a much-loved soup-base in France.

Sorrel Soup

To three pints of water add about 1 lb. of sorrel leaves, chopped coarsely, bring to the boil, and simmer for about 10 minutes. Cool slightly, and add a beaten egg, thinning it first with some of the liquid. Chill well. At serving time, put 1 tablespoon of sour cream, thinned with some of the soup, into each serving. You can garnish with slices of hard-boiled egg, or a twist of sour cream. If you cannot raise 1 lb. of sorrel from your garden. try making a third of the quantity. This should be enough for 4 people.

An unusual sauce for fish, poultry or white meat can be made with French sorrel and other greens.

Green Sauce

Cook the leaves of sorrel, watercress and lettuce with a small whole onion (remove this after cooking) in just a very little water, stirring till tender. Then add a tablespoon of olive oil, a tablespoon of vinegar, and pepper and salt to taste, stirring with a wooden spoon until it is like green cream. Delicious with pork.

The oxalic acid, which was formerly called "salts of sorrel" is a blood cleanser. Taken in moderation in the diet it helps the action of kidneys and liver, and is said by many writers to "dissolve" kidney stones. The pulped leaves, heated in a little water, make a good poultice for boils and skin eruptions.

Vegetable Cocktail

Sorrel is a great blood-purifier. Use it with any vegetable juices, as in this green drink.

4 large sorrel leaves
8 sprigs parsley
1 apple cucumber
2 comfrey leaves
3 stalks celery

Wash the leaves thoroughly, chop them coarsely and put through the juicer. A pinch of vegetable salt may be added to bring out the flavour.

Southernwood

Artemisia abrotanum COMPOSITAE

The name "wormwood" is loosely applied to many members of the Artemisia group. The true wormwood (*Artemisia absinthium*) provides the extract, absinthin, which was dissolved in alcohol to make the fiery French absinthe. Incomplete knowledge of this herb led Pernod, in 1791, into his absinthe recipe. Although a solution of wormwood in water can be a tonic, appetite restorative, and general body toner and strengthener, in alcohol the herb can have a slow poisonous effect, producing delirium and disorientation, and sometimes permanent mental breakdown if it is taken to excess. The French Government, alarmed at its ill-effects, banned the use of *Artemisia absinthium* in absinthe, and the liqueur is now made using an extract of aniseed instead.

Wormwood is a powerful insect repellent, as is its milder relative, southernwood. A handy herb for town dwellers, because it will withstand smog and a grimy atmosphere, southernwood grows to a height of about 3 feet in a loose clump of long, hard stems feathered at the tops with dusty green. In spring and early summer yellowish flowers appear, and a tea that can be made from both flowers and leaves has been used to expel roundworms from animals and humans. A small handful of the leaves and flowering tops to a cup of boiling water is the usual dose. Sweeten it with honey to overcome the bitter taste.

Dry the leaves, crumble them, and store with woollens to keep the moths away. Its ether-like smell is repugnant to them. Southernwood tea is also prescribed when people are convalescing from the flu: it helps combat the bodily weakness and pains in the limbs suffered with this wretched illness. It can tone up the skin, too, and the extract, santonin, can be a helpful rub to sufferers from rheumatic aches.

Reputedly, no snake will ever enter a garden where wormwood or southernwood is planted. Legend says that wormwood sprang up along the path taken by the Serpent on his way out of Eden as a barrier to any return. It is certainly a native of Iran and surrounding areas below the 8,000-foot level. St John the Baptist's girdle in the wilderness was made from wormwood stems, and the name has become associated with bitterness and self-imposed discipline.

In humid weather, southernwood and wormwood can act as strong insect repellents in the garden. Moisture on their leaves releases the ether-like scent so unpleasing to insects. Amongst roses, southernwood can act like garlic chives, keeping aphis away.

Wormwood and southernwood will also grow well in the sooty grimy atmosphere of the cities, especially in industrial towns where the chemically-saturated air seems almost beneficial to these plants. Our ecologists might soon be handing out free plants of southernwood to provide a green barrier for the people who have to live in such areas. Seriously though, these Artemisias may hold the key to establishing a more breathable air in such conditions, as they absorb, recycle and purify the chemical-laden atmosphere.

Poor, crusted soil, and even rocky conditions, will not deter southernwood. It will withstand dryness, but naturally grows more green and thick with sufficient water. In very cold or frosty areas it may drop some of its leaves in the winter, but will shoot again with fresh young green when the warm weather returns.

Germination from seed can be difficult. I have never yet found just which sowing conditions it *does* like, trying many different approaches and seed from various sources: but the germination rate was always so low as to be quite disheartening. Woody stem cuttings are a far easier way to gain new plants. Take them in late spring or early summer, with a "heel" of the old stem attached.

Wormwood and southernwood are recommended to be grown in poultry runs for shade. The birds will not scratch at them and their insect-repelling oils will keep lice and other vermin away from the enclosure.

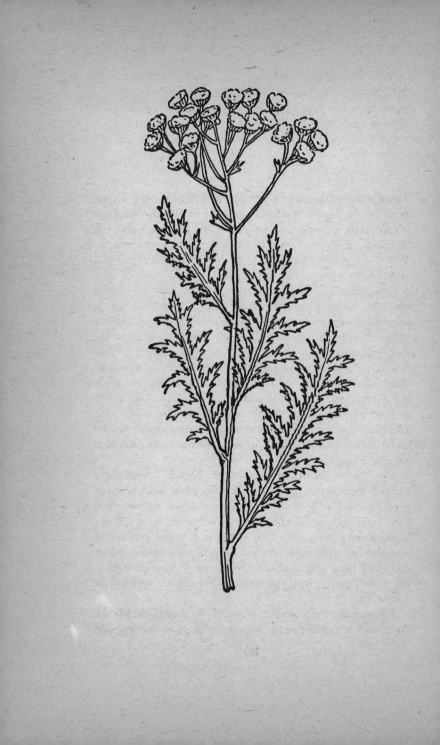

Tansy

Tanacetum vulgare COMPOSITAE

Tansy is one of the most mineral-rich of all herbs. It is a great plant for the organic gardener; its value in the compost heap is enormous. Bulging with potassium and assorted resins, oils and acids, its leaves provide many elements otherwise lacking. Whenever you cut back the plant (and cut it back you can, many times even in one season), strip the leaves from their fibrous stems, add half to the compost bin and mix it well through, and keep the other half to dry. Dried tansy leaves, rubbed between the fingers to release their pungent oil, can be scattered on pantry shelves to keep ants away. You can use the fresh leaves in spring and summer to keep your dog's coat flea-free. Rub a handful vigorously through the coat against the grain of the hair; the tanacetin oil is a flea, fly and other insect repellent. The dried leaves can be rubbed to a fine powder or pulverized in the blender and sprinkled around dog kennels or on the dog's blankets to keep insects away. Bruised tansy leaves, scattered across the path of an ant-trail, will send them scuttling for cover.

A highly medicinal herb of North English origin, tansy escaped from the monastery gardens to grow wild in many parts of Britain. Scottish and Irish traditional recipes often mention it, and the "drisheen", or blood pudding of County Cork, always contained a sprig of tansy. A bright yellow dye was obtained from the leaves, and this was often used to colour cakes and buns. Chopped tansy leaves can be used *sparingly* in cakes and pies, giving an unusual flavour as well as the colour.

A fresh tansy leaf was often placed in the shoe in the Middle Ages, and is credited with stopping cramps in the leg, and infection from the plague. This last sounds reasonable, for no insect or rodent would come near tansy-smelling feet.

Tansy is the easiest herb to grow. Just put one root into the most difficult spot in your garden, the spot where nothing will grow, and watch it thrive. It is a tall-growing plant (about 3 feet), with a wealth of deep-green, ferny leaves and heads of bright yellow "buttons" in summer, looking for all the world like daisies with all their petals missing. These flowers dry well if hung upside-down for several weeks, any leaves being first stripped from the stems, and are a quaint addition to any dried flower arrangement, keeping their bright yellow colour.

The name comes from the Greek *tanacetum*, immortality, and it was the legendary herb given by Mercury, on Jupiter's orders, to Ganymede to make him the gods' immortal cup-bearer. The "everlasting" qualities of tansy are attributable not only to the long life of its dried blooms, but also perhaps to its poisonous qualities if it is taken to excess. So use it only sparingly.

Culpeper had an abstruse comment to make about tansy; "Let those women that desire children love this herb; it is their best companion, their husbands excepted." Just how it was to be made use of, sadly he did not explain.

The leaves of tansy were often steeped in white wine and used as a regular face-wash to whiten the skin.

> *On Easter Sunday be the pudding seen*
> *To which the tansy lends her sober green.*

A tradition dating from Jewish rituals at Passover spread in England to become a country habit at Easter. Tansy, one of the first herbs to spring into growth after the winter snows, was used to flavour the Easter pudding, symbolizing the return of life and warmth to the soil. On a more mundane level, its use is ascribed to helping to rid the body of the wind-producing foods of Lent.

Here is the recipe. I have tried it, and am still not sure whether I like it. Unfortunately, no quantities were given to me in the original recipe which was a "throw-in" family one; so I have had to experiment.

184

Tansy Pudding

To a ¼ lb of ground almonds add flavouring essence such as lavender or rose, then add some soft breadcrumbs, grated nutmeg, a spoonful of brandy, a couple of tansy leaves, chopped, 3 oz. fresh butter and slices of lemon. Pour over it one pint of scalded milk (with a little sugar added to taste), and when cold mix all well together. Then add a few drops of lemon juice and 4 well-beaten eggs. Bake in a warm to moderate oven till set (about 1 hour).

Tansy flowers can be added to flour, about 1 dessertspoon to a pound, to give it an unusual tang, and a yellow colour. It is advisable to pulverize the flowers in the blender first. Grown under fruit-trees, tansy can repel the fruit moth, and it spreads and grows so fast that a green barricade can be put up in an orchard in one season.

To increase your supply of plants, dig the clump at the end of summer, separate the new growths from the root stem, and replant. Or leave it till the spring, and divide the clump as new growth starts from the base. This hardy herb will take to street-planting or anywhere you need an undemanding tenant of your soil. Insects will never attack it, but young snails like to hide in the leaves and may nibble new young growth if allowed to remain.

Don't forget: always bruise or rub the leaves to release tansy's insect-repelling oils.

Tarragon

Artemisia dracunculus COMPOSITAE

French tarragon is an almost purely culinary herb, having very little folk-lore or tradition behind it. Its bitter-sweet delicate flavour seems to typify the essence of French cuisine, although the plant was originally taken from Russian stock. Russian tarragon is reputed to be hardier and more vigorous and to have a stronger taste; but my own experience with French tarragon has proved to me that time spent in preparation of a good home for it in open sunshine can see it grow so abundantly as to rival its Russian parent in size without any loss of flavour delicacy. Experimenting with French tarragon, I put one small plant in early spring in a deeply dug bed, with blood and bone well under its roots and a soil rich in natural compost, in full open sunshine, and gave it plenty of water in the early settling-in period. Before the end of the summer, the bush was 2 feet high and 4 feet across, and some fifty-odd new plants had been dug and potted out from around its base. So I smile when told that French tarragon grows small and weedy.

In another part of the garden, in the partial shade of shrubs, but in otherwise similar conditions, I then planted a second tarragon. Sure enough, it grew thin and straggly as the books had foretold. It seems that in warmer climates tarragon can have, and indeed should have, the open sunshine not recommended for it in English and Continental conditions. I have since proved to my own satisfaction that this is so. Tarragon should be in your sunniest herb bed, with room to cascade sideways if it wishes. Leave an area about four feet across when setting it out in the garden. With well-fed soil, it should fill this space before the end of one growing season.

Tarragon can easily be dried. Pick the long woody stems at

the height of their late summer or autumn growth, tear off the trailing side branches and dry these; or slice off the top, soft growth with shears, and spread it out on racks. Strip the leaves from the stems when brittle and crackly, and store as usual.

A delightful herb vinegar can be made by steeping a large handful of the soft tops in wine vinegar for a week. Remove the herb, and if a stronger flavour is required, repeat with new leaves for another week.

The mature bush may die right back in winter in cold or frosty areas. Cut off the top growth, and cover the roots with a mulch of straw or peat moss for the winter, and the new root suckers will break through in the spring. These can be divided from the parent with a sharp spade or trowel, and replanted elsewhere. Indeed, it is advisable to keep new plants coming on each season, for the flavour is fresher and more concentrated in the new growth.

For the table, some of these following recipes should give you new ways to use this herbal aristocrat. Never use tarragon in soups or dishes needing a long boiling time: it becomes quite bitter and unpalatable.

Tarragon Sauce

Make a roux of 1½ oz. butter, 1 oz. flour, and add ½ pint of milk or stock, 1 shallot, and a handful of chopped tarragon leaves. Simmer for several minutes.

Ravigote Sauce
(*for chicken or other poultry*)

1 cup brown stock
1 tablespoon each chopped tarragon, chervil, chives
1 crushed garlic clove

Pour all into the roasting pan after removing the fat, but leaving all the juices, and bring just to the boil. Serve with the herbs still in. This can also be used on spaghetti, with grated cheese.

Tongue with Tarragon

2 to 3 lb. sliced tongue (cut thin)
2 tablespoons chopped tarragon
1 tablespoon capers
1 tablespoon cornflour, dissolved in 3 tablespoons water
½ cup stock, or bouillon
½ cup red wine
Crushed anise seed

Butter a shallow baking-dish, and arrange sliced tongue in several layers, sprinkling capers and tarragon between. Combine the stock and cornflour on the stove, stirring till smooth. Add salt and pepper if necessary. Add crushed anise seed and red wine to mixture, then pour it over the tongue and bake for 30 to 40 minutes, or until the sauce catches at the side of the pan.

French Mustard

3 tablespoons dry mustard, mixed to a paste with cold water or white wine. Add ½ teaspoon sugar, 1½ teaspoons tarragon vinegar, ½ teaspoon salt, 1½ teaspoons safflower oil, ¼ teaspoon pepper. Mix all together, in blender if possible, to give it the true creamy texture.

Thyme

Various varieties LABIATAE

An anonymous English poet wrote in 1799,

> *Thick-growing thyme, and roses wet with dew*
> *Are sacred to the sisterhood divine.*

Thyme has always been associated with female ailments, and is symbolic of the devotion of motherhood. It also stands for courage and strength. It was a favourite Roman herb, brought initially from Attica to provide beehives with its rich pollen. The common *Thymus vulgaris* is supposed to provide bees with the best raw-material in the plant world for their honey-making.

All the many varieties of thyme are edible, all are valuable medicinally, and all are perennial and evergreen. Originally natives of sun-drenched, rocky, mountainous districts, they thrive in courtyards, paths and rockeries, asking very little in the way of feeding; but they must have heat and good drainage to produce the tiny starry flowers typical of them all.

These herbs were all placed under the sign of Aries, the warm-blooded, and their antiseptic properties were used freely by earlier civilizations. Thymol, the oil that all members of the mint family contain, is present in very concentrated amounts, and the pure oil is an antiseptic twelve times as powerful as carbolic acid. You can make a milder thyme oil yourself as described on p. 26. This can be used whenever a headache strikes. Instead of reaching for drugs and sedatives, try some of Nature's balm instead. Rub a few drops of the oil into your temples or wherever the headache is worst, and let its warmth and pleasing scent soothe your psyche. So simple, so economical, and so effective! Thyme oil should also be available through natureopathic suppliers or your health store. The milder oil can be used as an antiseptic to rub on cuts or grazes, too.

Sorting out all the varieties of thyme can be a headache to the botanist. They hybridize freely and lose their individuality in the process. However, some of the more common species which remain fairly true to type are listed below.

GARDEN THYME (*Thymus vulgaris*) An erect-growing tiny shrub, with dark green leaves and woody stems. Strong flavour, produces the best oil.

LEMON THYME (*Thymus citriodorus*) A lovely lemon-scented type, delicious with all meats, and a strong grower. Pink flowers in spring and summer.

CARAWAY THYME (*Thymus herba barona*) A native of Corsica. Rich caraway perfume when crushed, and a trailing creeping habit, rooting as it spreads.

Creeping thymes come in a multitude of types, the grey woolly thyme with its furry bluish-grey leaves and pale flowers; Shakespeare thyme, growing in a little cushion of light green; the white and pink-flowered *Thymus serpyllum* for small lawns in a sunny spot; and many others. Each will cover a large area in quite a short time, particularly if reflected heat from rocks and stones can reach it.

Light soil suits all the thymes best, but they will grow in heavier soils if necessary. Don't feed them too much; poorer conditions suit them better. Artificial fertilizers can even be fatal to them, or at best can cause leaf-drop and yellowing of the remaining foliage. Thyme is the poor man's herb: it will just grow and grow and grow.

Thyme tea is often prescribed for sore throats and colds. Take a good handful of the fresh herb, pour a cup of boiling water over, let it stand for a few minutes, and then sip slowly. Taken internally this way, the antiseptic thymol can kill many germs and bacteria in the throat and respiratory passages.

On the culinary side, thyme stands as one of the Big Four, which include sage, parsley and marjoram, these being used together in a *bouquet garni* for flavouring soups, stews and hot-pots. Its best-known use is to flavour grilled, roasted or broiled meat, but it can be a vegetable "flavour-saver" too. The Romans used it with soft cheese, and in liqueurs.

Chicken with Thyme

Season a small roasting chicken inside and out. Roast uncovered in a moderate oven for half an hour on each side. Remove the fat from the pan and add 1 whole lemon, cut into small cubes, ¼ cup of dry white wine, 2 tablespoons of redcurrant jelly, and several chopped stalks of lemon thyme. Return to the pan, and roast until tender. Serve this dish with whole fresh apricots, stoned, cut, and filled with horseradish and cream cheese. This makes a real special-occasion dinner.

Stuffed Cutlets

1 cup toasted stale bread, diced
½ cup sautéed chopped mushrooms
2 shallots, chopped and sautéed
Chopped thyme, pepper and salt
1 egg yolk to bind it all together

Cut pockets in chops or cutlets, insert the mixture and fasten with a toothpick. Brown the meat in a little oil, and transfer to a covered casserole, baking in a moderate oven for 20 or 25 minutes. Stir in ¼ cup of cream, and pour some of it over the chops. Reheat and serve immediately.

When roasting a loin of lamb, put salt, pepper, and chopped garden or lemon thyme between the chops. Cook a sprig of thyme with marrow and zucchini, and put a few leaves with mushrooms. In nineteenth-century France, thyme was used with many vegetable dishes; and seasoned stuffed tomatoes, a favourite of the southern provinces, were often flavoured with crushed thyme leaves.

The plants can easily be increased by dividing a clump and setting out again any rooted portions. Garden thyme grows easily from seed, too. Sow it in the spring or autumn. It will grow slowly for a while, but there is flavour and aroma in even the tiniest sprig, so use it right from the start.

Valerian

Valeriana officinalis VERBENACEAE

An unassuming, small herb, valerian gives very little outward evidence of the value it has always had in herbal therapy. You might pass it by altogether and not comment on its tufts of droopy light-green leaves. Even the flower stems are not really attractive, looking anaemic and skinny, with a pale head of creamy pink tiny blooms in the late spring.

Valerian has two important qualities: the strong sedative powers in its roots; and its ability to stir up and increase phosphorus activity in the soil around it, and provide rich mineral content for the compost bin.

The herb has been known and used for thousands of years. Sedative plants are rare amongst common herbs, and if your diet is right and you live as naturally as possible, if you are happy in your work or in the home and life is not too frustrating, you should never need a sleeping draught made from valerian root. However, illness involving severe pain, an accident, or any crisis that keeps you worried or tense so that sleep will not come night after night: all these depleting circumstances can find you in dire need of a safe, natural sedative like valerian.

Valerian grows on banks and near stone if possible, and Chaucer called one variety "Setewale", wryly commenting on its rather unpleasant odour and taste. Nature has put out her warning signals here, so don't use this herb lightly. Unlike sleeping pills and many synthetic drugs, valerian will cause neither addiction nor side effects, and it does not have narcotic properties. There is no immediate effect—you do not fall asleep five minutes after the first dose; it has a slower far-reaching action, promoting healthy nerves that do not feel the slings and arrows so much. Once again, natural medicine reaches not only the symptoms but the *cause* of the bodily discomfort, the jangled nerve centres sending frantic, anxious signals instead of calm relaxed ones.

Valerian likes its roots cool, but its foliage warm, and this seems to explain its liking for growing near stone. It will grow from seed planted in the spring. Just press down the seed gently on top of the damp soil, do not cover it, for it needs the warmth at this stage. Germination can be slow, and usually only about half of the little seeds sown will send their shoots through the soil. The root suckers (strictly speaking it is a rhizome, not a root) can be separated in late summer or autumn and replanted if you need more. Keep the flowering stems nipped off if you want to use the root only; it will have more strength. The mature rhizome can be dug in the autumn of the second growing season. This is a hazardous process if you own a cat: it can be sent into an almost delirious state of intoxication by the strong smell from the freshly dug root. After you have fought off any drunken cats, slice the root in slivers and put these on your screens in some out-of-the-way corner where its putrid smell when drying will not cause too much comment. If there are rats about, they will also come to the smell, and canny rat-bait manufacturers often mix dried valerian root with their poisons. Indeed, the Pied Piper is supposed to have lured the rats with a piece of valerian root as well as his magic music.

When dry, the root slivers can be powdered or pulverized in a blender and stored in glass jars to make a sedative tea. One teaspoonful of the powder to a cup of warm milk can be taken each day, the milk will help to disguise the strong flavour. Add a little honey if you like.

I can hear you saying, "Why should I drink a nasty brew like that when a clean pink sleeping pill will have a quicker effect?" The answer surely is in what *other* effects each one will have. Sleeping pills can make you feel dizzy and vague the next day, and do not really attack the cause of your problem; they only palliate the nerves by anaesthetizing them. They cost a lot, and you may find you need an ever-increasing dose to produce the same effect, with the possibility of permanent addiction. Nature's way costs you only a small amount of time and virtually nothing in cash. You will have no side-effects (provided of course you apply commonsense and take only this recommended quantity), and it will *strengthen* the nerves, not anaesthetize them. Valerian's high silica content and its natural phosphorus, too, will ensure this. If you don't want to wait two years before having your own supply, plant your valerian and get your intermediate requirements from your natureopath or health food store.

Obviously, Mercury is given dominion over this herb: it acts on the whole nervous system and the senses too, the "communicators" of the body. It is sometimes used in herbal treatment of epilepsy, and in other diseases of a mental or hysterical origin, where nerve "messages" are not getting through correctly. Its other ancient name, "All-heal", should speak for itself.

The pure valerian oil can be used externally for spinal rubs in diseases where the spinal cord needs stimulation or lessened sensibility to pain.

For the home gardener—plant valerian near vegetable rows, and use its cut tops and any small root remains in the compost. Its high phosphorus content seems to draw earthworms to the area, and this has been confirmed in field studies in America.

Keep valerian out of the kitchen, though. No culinary masterpiece can ever be created by the addition of a little valerian root powder.

Yarrow

Achillea millefolium COMPOSITAE

It is fitting that I finish my list of herbs with yarrow. It seems to me to typify the silent strength possessed by herbs in the healing of many ills, pulling the warmth of the sun and the welcome rain down into the soil to change by Nature's alchemy into natural minerals, vitamins and oils in the service of man. I stand beside my yarrow clump with a feeling almost of awe. The "sacred herb" of some of the earliest cultures of man, unchanged for thousands of years, grows in my garden with the same properties now as it had then. The Druids used yarrow stems to divine the weather for each coming season, and according to the ancient writings, their predictions were more accurate than those of our satellite pictures of today. Yarrow was one of the nine Anglo-Saxon sacred herbs, used in rituals and for protection from evil. Knowledge of the plant's strengths rather than superstition or magic must have been the basis of this ritual. Yarrow tea can be taken to relieve all bodily weaknesses caused by infectious diseases like colds and flu, or any prolonged debilitating illness. It is very often mixed with other herbs to strengthen the mixture and speed up its work. What more logical, then, than to say that yarrow wards off the "evil" of illness, which was always attributed then to unknown occult powers?

Hot yarrow tea, made from a handful of the fresh leaves, can break the most stubborn cold if taken each night on retiring. Two doses should be all you will need. It can also prevent cramp after exercise in cold weather, and can bring down a fever if taken very hot.

Much herbal lore was discovered originally by observing how animals included various plants in their diet to suit their body's requirements, and yarrow was found to be a favourite pasture food for cattle if seasonal changes or meagre grass pasture had weakened the herd. It also has a deflammatory action on swollen tissues of any kind, and was the herb supposedly used by Chiron the Centaur to cure the heel wound of Achilles. For its services on the battlefield in early times, it was called "Wound-wort" or the "Soldiers' Herb". Stitching a ragged arrow- or spear-gash was unheard of; so yarrow was used to reduce the swelling of the surrounding tissue, enabling the wound to close naturally, and heal. Fresh leaves were often packed straight into the torn flesh, there to staunch the flow of blood as well; and yarrow collected two more names, "Staunch-grass" and "Sanguinary". Next time your husband cuts himself while shaving, rush out to the herb garden for a yarrow leaf and press it firmly against the spot.

For a nose-bleed which will not stop, take a cup of yarrow tea. This will also promote appetite, and can be of assistance in any pelvic troubles.

One yarrow-taker wrote, "It has a beneficient effect, similar to that of a life on the ocean-wave in rough and stormy weather." This (I hope) was not to say, "It made me vomit", but referred to the breezy bracing strength a cup of yarrow tea can provide.

If I have one of those days when it becomes apparent that even getting out of bed was a mistake, on goes the red light saying: "Yarrow tea!"

For the gardener, yarrow pairs off with comfrey as a compost activator. In the chapter on Soil Fertility, I have mentioned the homoeopathic dose of yarrow for the compost heap. It is a natural vegetable activator that can halve the time taken for a bin of decomposing bits and pieces to become rich black compost. One or two of the tiny leaves, snipped small and mixed well through, can "send off" between one and two cubic yards of compost. The staggering chemistry involved in this process alone should give us great respect for yarrow.

Yarrow is beloved by homoeopathic physicians. A fresh leaf of yarrow pressed high up into the nasal passage can *cause* a nose-bleed and thus relieve the pressure of some types of migraine. A homoeopathic dose of yarrow can *staunch* a nose-bleed. Let a qualified homoeopath deal with these processes; they can be tricky if not properly understood.

The plant itself is a showy thousand-leaved tufted clump, throwing up flowering stems in spring and sometimes right through the summer, bearing Schiaparelli-pink heads of tiny daisy-like blossoms. There is a white variety, too, the pink being a "sport" from this pastureland and meadow kind. Hill, an old English herbalist, says "When accidents of growth give a blush of red to the flower, it would be thought, if found in America, a glorious acquisition to our gardens." Because it grows like a weed in Europe and Britain is no reason to exclude it from a flower garden. I find its spring and summer appearance most attractive, and in autumn and even winter new suckers spread out from the base of the clump and can be potted or planted elsewhere.

Yarrow is seldom troubled by insect pests, although the occasional grasshopper or snail may in desperation try a few of the young leaves if not much else is available.

There are several varieties suitable to grow in the herb garden. *Achillea millefolium* is the best medicinally, but there is also a small yellow-flowered kind, *Achillea tomentosa*, with greyish-green leaves in a miniature cushion, and *Achillea magna* with stiffer bigger leaves of a pale green, a most attractive plant.

Yarrow will enhance the flavour, strength and health of other herbs grown near it.

Footpath Philosophy

When my sons were young and going to kindergarten, my friends and I often sorted out all our own and the world's troubles standing on the footpath beside a car-load of impatient children waiting to be taken to or from. We were christened the "footpath philosophers".

The knowledge of herbs and their uses I have gained since that time has changed altogether some of the views I held then. No longer does it seem so important to "get on in the world". Now I feel that a natural and satisfying existence can be more readily attained by sacrificing much of the technology and artificiality of that life presented to us as "good" in our constant exposure to advertising and economic pressure.

Do we have to consume foods with all the vitality processed out of them, because we have never bothered to find out for ourselves the nutritional gap between them and natural foods? (It's so easy to open a packet!) Do we have to take pills and potions blindly, without inquiring into their long-term effects and the unnatural body balance they create? Doctors are not really to blame. They can prescribe only what is available and publicized to them by the drug and chemical companies, who, after all, are not philanthropic organizations, but competitive businesses required by their shareholders to make a sizeable profit. How many times has someone said to you, "The pills I had to take made me feel worse than the disease did in the first place."

Natural herbal therapy, applied with knowledge and understanding, never harms the human body. Its whole aim is to restore the balance of all the bodily functions and to eliminate the poisonous harmful wastes that cause illness. These poisons are often built up because the diet is deficient in natural minerals or vitamins. Herbs work in the *prevention* of illness.

If you have read the preceding chapters, you must now wonder what to plant with what, when to sow and when to harvest. Take it slowly; try to pick out just half a dozen herbs that appeal to you; plant them and learn about them gradually. Use them as often as possible in your diet and for simple home remedies if feeling off colour. You will soon want to add more to your collection.

The initial outlay in buying small plants or seeds, some dolomite, blood and bone, and a few simple tools, is all your herbs should ever cost you. My thrifty Scottish ancestors would be delighted to see the money I save. Not only do we not have to go to doctors, chemists and slimming classes: the herbs provide rich compost for the improvement of our soil, and additions to various recipes that enable us to live like gourmets on the free produce from our own garden. Gifts, like herb oils and vinegars, pot-pourri, or sweet and savoury jellies, can be made inexpensively for friends and relatives; and even shampoos and skin-toning preparations need only herbs and a few other simple ingredients you can easily put together.

Many times have people said to me, "Why aren't we *told* about things like this?" I should like to see a course on natural health and nutrition taught in the schools, particularly to girls who will influence their family's choice of foodstuffs in later life; and I feel that highly qualified natureopaths and homeo-pathic physicians should be recognized by medical doctors as partners, not competitors. Most study far longer, and are almost fanatically devoted to maintaining the health and well-being of their patients. Illness, that unnatural state of man, is, after all, their common enemy.

As yet, treatment from a natureopath is not recognized as treatment by a "qualified" medical practitioner; and this has reduced the ranks (and the incomes) of many men and women dedicated to healing. It has also reduced the numbers of their patients, as many who would like to have the benefit of this type of medicine cannot afford to pay the costs. Surely, these are two branches of the same science and should be recognized as such; one using artificial means and one natural means.

Theoretically (and logically) those using *artificial* methods should be tagged as "witch doctors" if that title is to be placed anywhere. Please don't think I have any grudge against medical practitioners. I believe only that they have been misled by the man-made "wonder drugs" of the last half-century, and by their patients' demand that the *symptoms* of illness should be cured as quickly as possible. Suppressing the symptoms only aggravates the body's inability to expel any disease-caused poisons. A runny nose is not pleasant, but it is the body's way of freeing swollen tissues from the waste matter accumulated in them.

Perhaps we ourselves are to blame. No one likes to be sick, and if illness strikes we would all like a magical potion to make us instantly well again. Tackle it from the other angle: use the goodness of herbs and natural foods to build up resistance and vital health, and disease will have trouble gaining a foothold. If it does lay you low, try rest, patience and Nature's remedies, and the *cause* of the illness should soon disappear.

On the lighter side, herbs can be fun. If you like to practise oneupmanship, do it with a drop of this and a sprig of that in your food when friends and relatives come for a meal. Keep them guessing, and surprise them with your skill.

So all I can add now is the phrase with which I ended my Introduction to these pages about the fascinating world of over twenty centuries of herbal lore:

Bon appétit, good health, and happiness!

Bibliography

Department of Agriculture, N.S.W., *Building up Fertility in the Garden*, 1966.

Aresty, Esther B, *The Delectable Past*. Allen & Unwin, London, 1965.

Bayne-Powell, Rosamund, *Housekeeping in the 18th Century*. John Murray, London, 1956.

Beeton, Isabella, *Cookery and Household Management*. Ward, Lock, London, 1960.

Berg, Sally and Lucien, *New Food for All Palates*. Gollancz, London, 1967.

Bethel, May, *The Healing Power of Herbs*. Wilshire Book Co., California, 1970.

Binding, G. J., *About Organic Gardening*, Thorson Publishers, London, 1970.

Brown, Alice Cook, *Early American Herb Recipes*. Tuttle, Rutland, Vermont, 1966.

Clarkson, Rosetta, *Herbs, Their Culture and Uses*. Macmillan, New York, 1942.

Clarkson, Rosetta, *Magic Gardens*. New York, 1939.

Claus, Edward P., and Tyler, Varro E., *Pharmacognosy*. Henry Kimpton, London, 1965.

Coates, Peter, *Flowers in History*. Weidenfeld & Nicolson, London, 1970.

Coats, Alice M., *Flowers and their Histories*. Black, London, 1968.

Cocannouer, Joseph, *Weeds, Guardians of the Soil*. Devin-Adair, New York, 1964.

Conarty, James, *Australian Intense Vegetable Culture*. Albert & Sons, Perth.

Culpeper, Nicholas, *Complete Herbal*. W. Foulsham, London.

Doole, Louise E., *Herbs, How to Grow and Use Them*. Garden Book Club, London, 1962.

Fitzgibbon, Theodora, *A Taste of Ireland*. Dent, London, 1968.

Grigson, Geoffrey, *A Herbal of All Sorts*. Phoenix House, London, 1959.

Hemphill, Rosemary, *Fragrance & Flavour*. Angus & Robertson, Sydney, 1961.

Hemphill, Rosemary, *Penguin Book of Herbs and Spices*. Penguin Books, 1966.

Hemphill, Rosemary, *Spice & Savour*. Angus & Robertson, Sydney, 1964.

Hills, Lawrence D., *Fertility without Fertilizers*. Henry Doubleday Research Association, Braintree, Essex.

Hills, Lawrence D., *Pest Control without Poisons*. Henry Doubleday Research Association, Braintree, Essex.

Hunter, Beatrice Trum, *Gardening without Poisons*. Hamish Hamilton, London, 1965.

Kirschner, H. E., *Nature's Healing Grasses*. A. C. White Publications, Riverside, California, 1970.

Levy, Juliette de Baïracli, *Herbal Handbook for Everyone*. Faber & Faber, London, 1966.

Levy, Juliette de Baïracli, *Herbal Handbook for Farm and Stable*. Faber & Faber, London, 1963.

Leyel, Mrs C. F., *Cinquefoil*. Faber & Faber, London, 1957.

Leyel, Mrs C. F., *Compassionate Herbs*. Faber & Faber, London, 1967.

Leyel, Mrs C. F., *The Magic of Herbs*. Jonathan Cape, London, 1932.

Loewenfeld, Claire, *Herb Gardening*. Faber & Faber, London, 1964.

Lucas, Richard, *Nature's Medicines*. Wilshire Book Company, California, 1970.

Lust, Benedict, *About Herbs*. Thorson Publishers, London, 1961.

McDonald, Christina, *Garden Herbs for Australia and New Zealand*. A. H. & A. W. Reed, Melbourne, 1960.

Macleod, Dawn, *A Book of Herbs*. Duckworth, London, 1968.

Mayer-Browne, Elizabeth, *Australian Cooking for You*. Bles, London, 1969.

Mellor, Olive, *Complete Australian Gardener Illustrated*. Colorgravure Publications, Melbourne.

Milne, Lorus and Marjorie, *Living Plants of the World*. 1967.

Murmet, Felix, *Culinary, Scented and Medicinal Herbs*. Gundarene, N.S.W., 1955.

Nilson, Bee, *Pears Family Cookbook*. Pelham, London, 1964.

Norris, N. E., *Nutrition and Food Preparation for Australian Schools.* Hicks Smith, Sydney, 1969.

Nottis, P.E., *About Fruit, Vegetables and Salads.* Thorson Publishers, London, 1960.

Petulengro, Leon, *The Roots of Health.* Souvenir Press, London, 1968.

Philbreck, Helen, and Gregg, Richard B., *Companion Plants.* Stuart & Watkins, London, 1967.

Prevention (magazine), "Make Compost in 14 Days". Rodale Press, Herts, 1963.

Rohde, Eleanour Sinclair, *A Garden of Herbs.* Dover Publications, New York, 1969.

Rohde, Eleanour Sinclair, *Culinary and Salad Herbs.* Country Life, London, 1940.

Shepherd, Dorothy, *A Physician's Posy.* Health Science Press, England, 1969.

Simmonite, Dr, *The Simmonite-Culpeper Herbal Remedies.* W. Foulsham, London, 1957.

Step, Edward, *Herbs of Healing.* Hutchinson, London, 1926.

Taylor, Norman, *Plant Drugs that Changed the World.* Allen & Unwin, London, 1965.

Wallis, T. E., *Textbook of Pharmacognosy.* Churchill, London, 1967.

Wannan, Bill, *Bill Wannan's Folk Medicine.* Hill of Content, Melbourne, 1970.

Woodward, Marcus, *Leaves from Gerard's Herball.* Bodley Head, London, 1943.

Index

Claire Loewenfeld and Philippa Back
Herbs For Health and Cookery £1.25

'While herbs have never lost their romantic appeal to the
imagination we have tended to forget their practical uses . . . For
those who would like to be more adventurous in their use and
knowledge of herbs, however, there is no better encyclopaedia
on the subject' SCOTSMAN

'A wealth of information on herbs and how to use them'
SHROPSHIRE STAR

'If you have a garden, then you should rope off a bit for herb
growing and buy the book immediately' NORTHERN ECHO

The Complete Calorie Counter 30p
with an introduction by Eileen Fowler

Did you know that 2oz of cottage cheese is worth 66 calories,
but the same amount of peanuts is worth 342 ? This invaluable
guide shows you at a glance exactly how many calories you will
take in. More calories equal more weight so count the calories
and watch the scales go down.

Antony & Araminta Hippisley Coxe
The Book of the Sausage £1

The incredible history of the Sausage — from Ancient Rome to
the Succulent Seventies . . . the A to Z of the Sausage — from
Alpenkluber to Zampone . . . the Gastronome's geography of
the Sausage . . . the arts of complete do-it-yourself sausage-
making . . . how to serve and enjoy the banger plus a guide to
drinking with Sausages . . .

Enrica and Vernon Jarratt
The Complete Book of Pasta £1.25

Heaped with authentic Italian sauces, or delicious simply with
parmesan and butter melting over it, the enormous range of
pasta has long been the staple ingredient of Italian kitchencraft.
The Jarratts, Rome's most famous restaurateurs, guide you
through the ways to make your own pasta and prepare the
traditional and mouthwatering sauces to complete the dish in
real Italian style.

'A boon to British cooks' TIMES LITERARY SUPPLEMENT

Kenneth Lo
Cheap Chow 80p

Chinese Cooking on next to nothing. Kenneth Lo is Britain's
leading Chinese gourmet and cookery writer and he admits
that some of the best Chinese eating he's known has been in
bedsitters where funds are short. His healthy diet is easy and
economical.

'For adventurous cooks . . . a must' HOUSE & GARDEN

George Lassalle
The Adventurous Fish Cook £1

Winner of the 1976 Glenfiddich Award for the best original
contribution to food cookery.

'Includes most things you want to know about the harvest of
our oceans and how to prepare, cook and serve it to the best
advantage' SUNDAY TELEGRAPH

Katie Stewart
The Times Cookery Book £1.75

Carefully chosen from the recipes published in *The Times* over the last few years and including many new ones, this collection of recipes by Katie Stewart is practical, varied and imaginative.

Selected to suit both everyday needs and special occasions, these recipes provide a rich source of new ideas for anyone who enjoys cooking.

Theodora FitzGibbon
A Taste of Paris £1.75

'Every food lover, every Paris lover, should buy this. The photographs have been skilfully chosen and are most evocative . . . La Mère Catherine in the Place du Tertre, the original Tour d'Argent, the late lamented Les Halles . . . pure nostalgia' GUARDIAN

'No cookery reference shelf would be complete without a collection of the books of that great cook Theodora FitzGibbon . . . dishes from French cookery that even the most humble of cooks can produce with ease . . .' SUNDAY TELEGRAPH